Young, Black, Rich, and Famous

The Rise of the NBA, the Hip Hop Invasion, and the Transformation of American Culture

Todd Boyd

With a new introduction by the author

University of Nebraska Press
Lincoln and London

First Nebraska paperback printing: 2008

Library of Congress Cataloging-in-Publication Data
Boyd, Todd.
Young, Black, rich, and famous: the rise of the NBA, the hip hop invasion, and the transformation of American culture / Todd Boyd; with a new introduction by the author.
p.   cm.
ISBN 978-0-8032-1675-4 (pbk.: alk. paper)
1. Basketball—Social aspects—United States.   2. Hip–Hop—Social aspects—United States.   3. United States—Race relations.   4. African American basketball players—Social life and customs.   I. Title.
GV889.26.B69   2008
796.323′640973—dc22
2007034948

Introduction to the Bison Books Edition

Most intellectuals will only half listen/so you can't blame jazz musicians/or
David Stern with his NBA *fashion issues.*
—Nas, "Hip Hop Is Dead" (2006)

At the end of 2006 that venerable wordsmith Nasir Jones, otherwise known as the rapper Nas, released his ninth solo album, the provocatively titled *Hip Hop Is Dead.* The album is indeed a masterpiece, especially considering the dismal state of hip hop in post-9/11 America. Nas embraces the tradition of the culture at the expense of the present state of the game, where commercialization, repetition, and an overriding lack of creativity have taken a toll on a once uniquely energetic and influential form of expression.

Nas's album incited a lot of controversy in hip hop circles for the boldness of its statement, particularly among southern rappers (who now seem to dominate much of what passes for hip hop), many of whom felt slighted by the title's implied dismissal of their more recent achievements. One could argue the album's assertion rings true on the basketball court as well. Quite a bit has happened in the intermingled worlds of basketball and hip hop since I began writing the first edition of *Young, Black, Rich, and Famous* back in the days immediately following the now infamous events of September 11, 2001. At the time, the inevitability of a profound connection between the two spheres of influence seemed to be a given, and this was what motivated the writing of the book in the first place.

The NBA, for a time, used hip hop to help market the game. Back then, young players directly out of high school were coming into the league in droves, bringing their own version of hip hop style and attitude with them. Now, players must be at least nineteen and a year out of high school before making the jump to the NBA. This move in and of itself is not necessarily a bad thing. I have long felt that the physical, mental, and emotional grind of NBA life is too much for a young player just out of high school. Though there have obviously been several phenomenal players who have made the leap over the years—KG, Kobe, T Mac, and LeBron immediately come to mind—players like this are the exception as opposed to the rule. Exposing young men to college has never hurt anyone, even if it's only for a year.

Nonetheless, even though this new age limit might not seem like a drastic or adverse change, it does mark one of several recent rulings that have altered the overt representation of hip hop's influence on the court. Because of these changes, what was once the era of the oversized throwback jersey worn by so many hip hop–minded players eventually morphed into the era of the ubiquitous white tee. Now, with these rules fully implemented, it appears that both eras have come to an end.

In 2005 NBA commissioner David Stern instituted a dress code, which forced players to get "suited," as they say, dropping the casual attire of hip hop for a more business-friendly look. These new dress code rules also applied to banning items such as fitted baseball caps and bling, staples of a balla's hip hop wardrobe. In addition to the condescending absurdity inherent in telling grown men what to wear, the invocation of a dress code was most certainly intended to mitigate the visual appearance of players who embraced hip hop style. This new rule furthered a long and complicated struggle between the league and the players over issues of style that dates back to the days when the original Air Jordan sneakers were banned in the mid-1980s.

Stern also began tightening the interpretation of the technical foul rule, giving the referees even more subjective power in handing out techs as they choose. Players are now suspended for one game after accumulating sixteen technical fouls in the regular season. The players are then suspended an additional game for every other tech accumulated after their sixteenth. I call this the "Rasheed Wallace Rule" because the colorful Pistons player is the person for whom the rule seemed to be created in the first place; he is also, no surprise here, the player who has been most affected by this ruling. Beyond Rasheed, though, the rule has the ability to give the players even less of a voice in objecting to on-the-court situations. Again the players are treated like little children as the articulation of their emotions has effectively been silenced in this regard.

Ironically enough, now it appears that Stern's exclusive focus on the players and the impact that they have on the league's overall image might have been at the expense of something much more damaging. While the commissioner had been busy micromanaging the players' wardrobe choices and attempting to stifle their sense of free expression on the court, it was revealed in the summer of 2007 that veteran NBA referee Tim Donaghy was guilty of betting on games that he officiated, along with providing insider information to gamblers for profit, in a scandal that cut to the core of the league's integrity. It will be interesting to see what long-term effects the fallout from this particularly egregious scandal will have on the game.

The combination of these new rules and the attitude that accompanied them helped to suck the life out of a vibrant sport in the league's attempt to make this urban game more palatable for an older, mainstream, suburban, White audience. At one point Stern even met with former Republican operative Matthew Dowd to inquire how the game might appeal to a red-state audience. It is not hard to imagine how incongruous a hip hop league would be to a Republican audience, but the fact that this was even a concern at all speaks volumes about the league's intent.

Most of these changes to the NBA came in the aftermath of that now infamous brawl that took place during the Indiana Pacers and Detroit Pistons game at the Palace of Auburn Hills in November 2004. The Pacers' resident lunatic Ron Artest jumped into the stands after being hit by a plastic cup thrown by a stupid-ass fan. Several members of the Pacers soon joined in, and the rest, as they say, is history.

Using the brawl as a self-fulfilling prophecy, many of the haters felt that the game had run amok, and much of the blame was laid at the feet of hip hop culture. It was suggested by many in the media that the brawl had been fueled by an overly violent hip hop disposition that informs the mindset of the modern-day player. While the incident had absolutely nothing to do with hip hop and everything to do with an emotionally unstable Artest, hip hop had become a convenient scapegoat for the masses, many of whom wouldn't have known what hip hop truly was even if it hit them in the face.

Similar claims were made about hip hop in the ruckus that surrounded radio host Don Imus when he referred to the Rutgers women's basketball team as a group of "nappy headed hoes" in 2007. Again the conversation shifted to hip hop as the culprit in this case, even though Imus had nothing to do with hip hop. Hip hop has obtained such a bad reputation now that I'm still surprised that no one has found a way to blame the genre for America's seemingly never-ending war in Iraq.

Yet for those of us who have come up in hip hop and who know the real deal, all these false charges have become par for the course. At its core hip hop has always been about the unfettered articulation of a Black male street perspective on life. This is why the culture linked up so well with the predominately Black male ethos of the NBA. In other words, hip hop and many of the Black players in the league spoke the same language and represented the same struggle. For this reason one can expect that there will always be a certain amount of tension due to the precarious place that Black men still occupy in American society.

Now it seems that the unique voice and undying struggle related to hip hop have come to at least a temporary end. Crushed by the dictates of both the David Stern–led NBA league office and the playa hatin' masses, the marriage of hip hop and 'ball appears to have gone the way of those old "booty" shorts that basketball players wore back in the 1980s.

Not so fast though. For all of this negativity and playa hatin', the spirit of hip hop continues to live on in the game of basketball and throughout American life. Hip hop has had far too strong an impact on our culture to die such an easy death. Notice, for example, LeBron James throwing up "the Roc" sign on the court after making a spectacular play. "The Roc," of course, represents the record and clothing label that is so closely connected with the persona of hustler-turned-rapper-turned-mogul Jay-Z, who also happens to be a part-owner of the New Jersey Nets. The point is that hip hop is embedded in the fabric of NBA culture, and even though the days of it overtly jumping out at you may have passed, this influence remains because hip hop has come to define a generation of people, both on the court and off.

The evolution of American culture in the post–civil rights era means that notions of blackness function quite differently now than was the case in the past. 'Ball and hip hop now exist firmly in the center of this overall culture, and as time goes forward we will continue to see the permanence of both forms.

Consider *Young, Black, Rich, and Famous* to be my own hip hop history of the modern NBA. To try and eradicate the influence of hip hop on 'ball and on other walks of life is a gigantic waste of time. Though hip hop has many detractors, and many of them happen to be Black, it can never be completely eliminated. You cannot kill the spirit and soul of hip hop, and this is what the players bring with them when they step on the court. The up-from-the-streets ethos of hip hop and basketball will provide strength and energy for a long time to come. Like most things that seep into our societal core, the influence itself might not always be so visible to the naked eye, but its essence will continue to inform the mind, body, and soul of this game we call basketball.

For the eagles,
who don't fly with sparrows

Acknowledgments

Once again it's on. Time to show love to those who have inspired, motivated, supported, indulged, and assisted me in my attempts to further cast my influence on the world. Shit is real in the field, no doubt!

Peace to Edward and Mozelle Boyd for the foundation and for taking me to my first NBA game. Peace to all my peeps: Patrick Smith, David Was, Kenneth Shropshire, Gil Friesen, Brian Smith, James Scott, Carl Fletcher, Sohail D., Larry Platt, Javier Jimenez, Albert Berger, Keith Westbrook (wherever you are). Hold it down, y'all. Peace to my agent Winifred Golden for recognizing the game in me. Peace to Emily Lacy and Lisa Allen for all your research and assistance. Peace to Janet Hill at Doubleday/Harlem Moon for recognizing my skills with the written word. Peace to Wayne Wilson at the Amateur Athletic Foundation for all those NCAA tapes. Peace to Ed Derse for hooking me up with Wayne Wilson. Peace to Billy Hunter and all the cats down at the NBA Players Association annual meeting in Puerto Rico, June 2002, for allowing me into your world, listening to what I had to say, and for feeling it the way you did. Game recognize game. Peace to all the streetballers and playground legends who set the standards but never got paid.

Finally, I say peace to all the imaginary playas and erstwhile playa haters who have tried to put salt in my game, stagnate my process, and stop my flow. You are the greatest motivators that I could ever ask for. Your arms too short to box with Todd! Please believe it. Stop hatin' and get your mind right!

Peace

Contents

Introduction
The Playa's Life

I consider myself quite fortunate. Life has granted me the opportunity to make a living by writing, lecturing, and thinking about things that I truly love; things like basketball, hip hop, movies, clothes, and money, among other things, and not necessarily in that order. See, I get paid to pontificate on what all these things really mean. When I'm watching a flick, a basketball game, a music video, whatever, I'm working. What for most people remains a leisurely activity, for me is a calling, a way of life. This is the way I ball.

When I was at the University of Iowa getting my PhD, they taught me something called critical theory. I am now employed in the division of Critical Studies. I say all this by way of explanation because people never seem to know what it is that I do. At Iowa they taught me the methods of theory and criticism. They also gave me an erudite language with which to articulate all this. They did not teach me how to be critical, though.

I learned how to be critical by growing up as a Black man in America, and that's something no university could ever teach me, no matter how intellectually rigorous. I picked up the game, as I like to call

it, in barbershops, on street corners, at the basketball court; hangin'
with niggas, choppin' it up, politickin', all day long.

Richard Pryor once talked about his father sitting in the barbershop, reading the almanac, and, in his words, "waiting for a muthafucka
to make a mistake." I can totally identify with that. The barbershop,
or anyplace else where Black men have been allowed to gather in numbers, has always been where some of the most sophisticated analysis was
being put forth, in a highly charged and colorful atmosphere to boot.
These moments are like a seminar, and I must say that the things I
learned in these situations often were more informative than the bull-
shit that I heard being disseminated in my graduate school classes.

This notwithstanding, I am an educated fellow. I suffered long
enough to get the PhD, and this is a part of my arsenal as well. This is
what I think makes me unique, actually. It is the ability to walk both sides
of the street, to move across boundaries like Dr. J used to move past defenders. I have known many people who spouted street wisdom all day
long, but they never made it off the street. I have also known an equal
number of people who have absorbed all the formal education that a
mind can consume, but who never moved outside of the ivory tower of
academia. I have tried to do both.

This is what I like to call the fusion of the formal and the vernacular.
It is my attempt to merge the style of a vibrant Black oral tradition with
the most sophisticated intellectual analysis. Imagine a cross between an
intellectual like Einstein and a supreme Black man like John Shaft (the
Richard Roundtree version, that is). I like to think of myself as equal
parts: scholar, gentleman, and nigga.

To those unhip to what it is that I speak, I am simply saying that as
an educated nigga, who has learned to master the King's English in a
very formal way, I have chosen to nuance that training with the lessons
that I have learned as a Black man in America. This is where 'ball and
hip hop come in. When I step into a crowded lecture hall, I approach
it as though I were walking into an arena. I prepare for the lecture like
I would practice for a game. I want to electrify the crowd like Michael
Jordan droppin' a double nickel on the New York Knicks only a few days

after coming back out of retirement. I want the words that come out of my mouth to be as precise as the lyrics that Biggie Smalls once let flow from his blessed tongue. My mouthpiece is platinum, and the words that come from it are like pearls of wisdom tricked off with a whole new flava.

———

As I'm writing this I hear the lyrics "I want to be free" playing on that soundtrack called my mind. These words come from a cat named Sugarfoot, who, if he were still singing today, would probably spell his name "Sugafoot," and more than likely he wouldn't be singing anyway, he'd be rappin'.

Sugarfoot, of course, was the lead singer of that great '70s band the Ohio Players, and his words echo the sentiments that have driven Black people forward ever since they jacked the first African and dropped his ass off in that unfamiliar 'hood known as America. Freedom, and the pursuit of it, in one form or another, is what life for Black people in America has always been about. "I wanna be free, say it Brotha!"

To me, basketball and hip hop are about seeking this same freedom. The freedom of expression, the freedom to exist on one's own terms, and ultimately, the freedom to do whatever the fuck you want! These twists on freedom underlie the quest inherent to both 'ball and hip hop for those who are young, Black, rich and famous in the modern world. This is their version of the American Dream. Whether they are on a basketball court, in the studio, or better yet, like my man Q said, back on the block, the quest is the same—freedom. This search for freedom though has taken place in a land where the penitentiary has often been the reality. Therefore this pursuit, this higher calling, is that much more aggressive.

When Vince Carter throws it down like his life depended on it, when Nas spits a perfect rhyme, or when I write evocative words on a digital page, it's all in pursuit of that elusive notion of freedom. Tryin' to get over is the way that both Mahalia Jackson and Curtis Mayfield put it. Mashin' for my ration, each and every day. This is what it's all about.

*Police pursued me / chased, cuffed, and subdued me /
talked to me rudely / cause I'm young / rich / and I'm
black / and live in a movie.*
— JAY-Z, "Blueprint (Momma Loves Me)"

I write the words in this book because I am tired of hearing guys like Bob Costas and George Will tell me about the significance of the game of baseball; a game that at its best is about as interesting as watching two snails run the marathon. Further, I say what I say because I have grown restless having to listen to Bill Walton, a man who once tested the bounds of free expression himself but is now often condemning in his commentary of those who comprise the young, Black, rich and famous. I am motivated in my words, thoughts, and deeds to provoke all those playa haters, Black, White, and otherwise, who want to see Black men lift that barge and tote that bale while walking the straight and narrow, making ever so sure to stay in their place.

I am charged with the mission of dominating your mind and liberating your soul, and I choose to do so with all the might of a Shaquille O'Neal dunk or the fury of Rakim's poetic lyrics. I start to think, and then I sink into the paper like I was ink.

The search for freedom for a Black man, even an educated one, in this place we call America is never dull and certainly not without drama. I love basketball and hip hop because they allow me to tap into the relative freedom that both afford. When the same system that once enslaved you now rewards you with a lifestyle that is both rich and famous, it is imperative that you take note. Pimp accordingly. Pimp the system that is. Get what you can, by hook or crook, and make 'em applaud you in the process. This is the cruel irony that now visits itself on the descendants of former slaves, and this is what I used as a backdrop when writing what you shall read here.

At the end of the day, this book is about so much more than basketball or hip hop. These are simply vehicles that help us get where we need to go. It's about how, when you are told to run through hell in gasoline draws, you still figure out a way to avoid getting burned, and even manage to run with a distinct style and grace in the process. It's about how America and the world have evolved since the 1980s and how Black popular culture is integral to understanding this evolution. It's about what Biggie Smalls called "money, hoes, and clothes." It's about all that is potentially right and wrong in the world. It's about time!

Peace,

The Good Dr.

LA, 4.03

Young,
Black,
Rich, and
Famous

Young, Black, Rich and Famous

'Ball, Hip Hop, and the Redefinition of the American Dream

The streets is a short stop / Either you're slingin' crack rock or you got a wicked jumpshot.

— THE NOTORIOUS B.I.G.
"Things Done Changed"

Not Guilty

One of my favorite items of clothing is a #3 Philadelphia 76ers jersey. This is, of course, the number that Allen Iverson wears on the basketball court. Whenever I wear this jersey it is guaranteed that I am going to hear all sorts of unsolicited comments from a range of people. Living in LA, I always get the Laker fans who think that I am in league with Philly. This was especially true during and after the 2001 NBA finals when the two teams met. This is minor though, because what I most often get are looks of disgust and comments that reek with judgment and moral indignation. "Why are you wearing that?" "Why do you wear *his* jersey?" "I hate him." These are just a few of the many hostile barbs that this jersey generates.

1

One day while walking on the USC track, I encountered a colleague of mine. He immediately launched into his own form of Iverson bashing, without prompt, mind you. "Allen Iverson? Well, he's not much of a team player, is he?" On another occasion I was set to speak at an academic conference and a female friend of one of my other colleagues came up to me and asked, straight up, "Why are you wearing a wife beater's jersey?" I was momentarily confused. What did she mean? I know that people now routinely refer to white tank top undershirts as "wife beaters" and so I thought that maybe because I had on a tank top, she thought it inappropriate attire for an academic conference and was using "wife beater" to refer to any tank top. No, this is not what she meant at all. She was referring to Iverson as a "wife beater," and I was surprised because I had never heard that he had been charged with such a crime. I guess I shouldn't have been surprised because people have accused him of everything else, so why not add "wife beater" to the list?

In the early days of July 2002 news broke that Iverson was being investigated for his involvement in a bizarre domestic ordeal. Iverson, supposedly, had gotten into an argument with his wife, Tawanna, put her out of the house, and later went to look for her at the apartment of his first cousin, whom his wife had left home with after the argument. As the allegations go, Iverson, upon not finding her at the apartment, forced his way in, revealed a gun tucked in his waistband, and proceeded to threaten the two men who were occupying the apartment, one of whom was his cousin's roommate. The Philadelphia police eventually issued a warrant for Iverson's arrest, charging him with fourteen criminal infractions ranging from gun possession and criminal trespass to making terroristic threats, among other things. Somehow this all got translated into "wife beater" for the inquiring female.

The minute someone accuses Iverson, he is immediately guilty in the minds of his detractors. As a matter of fact, he is already guilty, before even being charged. Never mind that eventually all those fourteen criminal charges against him were dropped. His critics choose to ignore that there was even a strong suggestion that extortion was at the root of these accusations. All of this notwithstanding, most people will remember the charges brought against Iverson, but few are probably even aware, nor do they care to be made aware, that all the charges were eventually dropped.

I wear the Iverson jersey, one, because I am a master agent provocateur, but more to the point because it is my form of protest against the racial profiling of another young Black man. I love the fact that he has become the nigga you love to hate on the basketball court. He is about as misconceived a figure as one could possibly imagine and, as I myself have found out, there is a certain "guilt by association" that comes with simply wearing his jersey. The Iverson haters see a reprobate, but these same people often fail to see his hard work when he plays through all sorts of pain and defies all odds as often the smallest man on the court in a sport dominated by height. His critics ignore his desire, his will to win, his pimp-or-die attitude toward the game he plays so well.

Many want Iverson to be a quiet, unassuming, passive, seen-and-not-heard negro who goes out and does whatever he's told and is grateful for the opportunity. Iverson though is a loud, boisterous, aggressive nigga who does not give a fuck and demonstrates his gratitude by parking his drop-top Bentley in the T.G.I. Friday's parking lot, blastin' hip hop, and hangin' with his boys.

There is a story that Reebok, Iverson's athletic-shoe sponsor, wanted some time with the star to film a new commercial during the NBA finals of 2001. As the story goes, Reebok felt that Iverson's likable counterpart, Kobe Bryant of the Lakers, was getting too much of the attention, as his Adidas commercials were seemingly on television all the time. Iverson though blew off several of the commercial shoots, and when questioned about why he would disregard something so important to his career and, more important, to his bank account, he reportedly told a close friend, "I give them muthafuckas a commercial every night. What the fuck else they want?" This supreme indifference to convention, taste, or standards is what makes Iverson such a lightning rod for controversy and a hero for hip hop.

———

WHEN THE ORIGINAL charges were levied, Iverson awaited the return of his lawyer from a European vacation so that he could surrender to

3

the police. During this wait Iverson was effectively put under house arrest by the authorities. Told not to leave home or be seen in public, or risk being apprehended, the notorious baller, in keeping with the dictates of hip hop culture, threw a lavish party at his home in full view of the media and the rest of the viewing world to help pass the time. This gesture was about as in-your-face as one could be, and especially true to form for the man often referred to as "The Answer."

This situation, of course, resonated throughout the culture as Iverson's immense success on the basketball court has consistently been contrasted against his problematic media image. Iverson has been labeled a thug since coming to the NBA in 1996. He has often been closely linked to hip hop culture as a part of this stereotyping. Iverson is as much a hip hop icon as he is a basketball player, and this has led to much contentiousness between the player, the media, and the sports establishment, who have found fault with the way he carries himself.

When the allegations arose, many, I am sure, loudly proclaimed an emphatic "I told you so!" Iverson has never tried to argue that he was anything other than what he had been labeled: a real nigga. In the parlance of hip hop culture, he has been intent on "keeping it real," being true to his calling, and remaining authentic, in spite of what others might say. Iverson has never been interested in providing a positive image nor has he been interested in altering his image to fit with what the media and others want of him.

He is a young Black man from an impoverished background whose close connection to the world of single-parent households, crack cocaine, and gun violence, along with other regular features of the ghetto, have continued to inform his life in spite of the fact that he is now a wealthy basketball player and visible celebrity. Iverson continues to hang out with many of his friends from back in the day. He dresses like a hip hop gangsta: multiple tattoos, a 'do rag, cornrows, and abundant platinum jewelry. Iverson even recorded a gangsta rap album which, though never released, caused a great deal of controversy nonetheless.

Throughout Iverson's career in the NBA he has had frequent run-ins with his coach, Larry Brown, and with members of the media. Iverson and Brown have publicly feuded over Iverson's supposed insubordination, including being late to practice or often not showing up at all on so many occasions. For this, Iverson is also unapologetic. During a press conference after his team was eliminated from the 2002 playoffs, Iverson even ridiculed a member of the sports media for chiding him on not going to practice. Iverson pointed out that his performance in games, which has always been outstanding, was what he should be judged by, not practice. Many took Iverson's comments as another indication that he was simply a thug in a basketball uniform, intent on breaking every rule possible and obeying no one in particular.

For all of these reasons Iverson has become the menacing face of a merger between basketball and hip hop culture that has angered many individuals. To these people Iverson is a thug who represents the worst possible image of a modern-day basketball player. He is considered selfish, arrogant, incorrigible, flamboyant, and he is always located against a backdrop of some potential criminal intent. His detractors see Iverson as someone who might just as well be out robbing banks or selling dope were he not so occupied with basketball. Therefore, his indictment on these criminal charges goes right along with the negative perceptions; guilty beyond a shadow of a doubt.

The excessive nature of the charges in this case became highlighted by the counts involving the making of terrorist threats. In the aftermath of September 11, the allegations of terrorism against Iverson reveal just how hyperbolic this particular indictment is. To equate Iverson's supposed actions with terrorism, even rhetorically, after witnessing the real terror of September 11, is not only irresponsible, it is unequivocally racist.

This situation also brings to mind the accusation of "maiming by mob" that Iverson was originally charged with back in 1993 when as a prominent high school athlete he was involved in a racial confrontation that resulted in a bowling alley brawl in his hometown of Hampton, Virginia. "Maiming by mob" was originally an offense included in an antilynching law, but here they flipped the script and used it to indict Iverson. Though the offense and Iverson's conviction were eventually overturned, he spent several months in jail before being pardoned by Virginia governor Doug Wilder. The presumption of guilt though has remained with him in the same way that the allegations of July 2002 will continually inform his representation.

Iverson will forever be guilty in the kangaroo court of American public opinion. The excessive trumped-up charges in both cases are at the core of a criminal justice system and a prison industrial complex intent on placing as many Black men as possible behind bars. The individuals in question are guilty by birth; their skin is their sin.

Iverson is a young Black man with a distinct ghetto sensibility, and he is damn proud of it, too. Like so many other young Black men of his generation, he has been stereotyped as a menace to society. Additionally, the media have made Iverson the example of what is wrong with sports today. The racial implications of this are not lost here either. There remains a certain contempt for young Black men in this society, especially those who have the financial resources that Iverson does. This contempt is pronounced when those in question not only have money, but refuse to act in accordance with the straitjacketed rules that society often imposes on its young, Black, urban male citizens.

Yet the Allen Iversons of the world use their money and elite status as a buffer between themselves and the rest of the world. They are, like that famous line from the Hughes brothers' film *Menace II Society*, "young, Black, and don't give a fuck."

This refusal to conform, and having the money to sustain this posture, is at the core of what I am calling the redefinition of the American Dream. For quite some time this clichéd notion of the American Dream—a house in the suburbs, 2.5 kids, a dog, and a white picket fence—was dangled in the faces of African Americans like a red cape in front of an angry bull, or better yet a cholesterol-filled buffet dinner placed in front of a starving man, only to be snatched away as he's about to eat. The American Dream for Black people was at best a pornographic tease and at worst a cruel and unusual joke that was never intended for them in the first place. This concept was bogus from the start, so any redefinition of this elusive notion is to be expected.

Why would Allen Iverson or anyone else who fit his description be overly concerned about maintaining social standards that were never intended for them in the first place? Why would one assume that simply because an individual had made some money and gained some recognition that they would now feel the need to embrace an idea that was otherwise thought to be out of their reach, beyond their grasp, and over their head? Iverson's ability to rise to the top of his game and in turn make large sums of money doing it, against all odds that he would even survive adolescence, is what defines his existence.

I see Iverson's hip hop disposition as a most appropriate one. The American Dream for Iverson and all others who subscribe to this hip hop ethos has to do with making money off of their immense talents, gaining leverage and visibility because of it, and then telling a hostile and often racist America to collectively kiss their "young, Black, rich and famous" asses in no uncertain terms. This sense of vengeance and retribution, marked by a colossal indifference to mainstream taste and coupled with the money that affords such freedoms, is the new American Dream, one redefined to suit the purposes of those who were excluded from the original version of this otherwise empty concept.

Mainstream society is critical of those who change or "go Hollywood" when they encounter wealth and good fortune, yet this is never extended to Iverson and his colleagues. Though Iverson refuses to change, he is criticized for this. Yet it is this authenticity that endears him to so many in the hip hop world, who find his plight and his disposition to be directly in line with their own beliefs. He is what he is, and the minute people stop trying to make him fit into a slot that he refuses to be pushed into, all of this nonsense will stop. Iverson is the epitome of young, Black, rich and famous. His connection to basketball and urban culture has most certainly allowed him to redefine the lingering notion of the American Dream. He has become the face of a generation of basketball players who shun the ways of old and are determined to push forward, doing things their own way and not conforming to any societal expectations.

Charge It to the Game

Allen Iverson is but one example of the way that basketball often becomes a stage where many of the social and cultural concerns relevant to issues of race and class in America are performed. (I will discuss the nuances of Iverson's image and persona in more detail in chapter 8 of this book.) Again, money and visibility are very important in this regard. Over time, certainly since the late 1970s, basketball has offered a dizzying array of examples that propel a wide range of important cultural discussions, discussions that might otherwise be swept under the rug.

I am convinced that, for instance, the implications of race surrounding Larry Bird and the Boston Celtics in the 1980s were closely linked with what was being undertaken by the Reagan administration at the time. Reagan created a hostile environment for racial progress, and this informed people's attitudes regarding Larry Bird as the newest version of "The Great White Hope." The untimely death of hoopster Len Bias in 1986 was such that it prompted heated debates about drug use in society at large. Michael Jordan's ascendancy as one of the globe's most popular icons is particularly suited to basketball's ability to translate across a broad geographical divide; the game's ability to speak multiple languages, if you will. Charles Barkley's declaration that he was not a role model revealed this notion to be a coded, modern-day version of what used to be described in the phrase a "credit to the race." The debate around this issue still draws heat from its volatile social chemistry.

Allen Iverson's persona, especially when contrasted against a basketball child of privilege like a Kobe Bryant, helped expose the fault lines of class as they pertain to what images are acceptable and what images are too threatening, both in basketball and in the larger society. The recent influx of foreign players into the NBA, set against the increasing youthfulness of Black players at home, forces a reconsideration of what constitutes America and who truly can be represented as Americans. This in turn alters what we see as the American Dream, and how contemporary circumstances might nuance our perceptions about how one might achieve this goal, or whether or not people are even pursuing it in the first place. All of these things come from the world of basketball since the late '70s, and these instances, along with a million more, provide the backdrop against which this book is set.

SOME WORLDWIDE SHIT

The other lingering component here is the way in which the game of basketball is especially connected to various issues inherent to urban culture over this period of time. Basketball has, since at least the late '70s, if not longer, been an ongoing tale of various cities. This urban aesthetic, to me, is what distinguishes the game from other sports like baseball and football.

Baseball, as America's national pastime, is just that, past time. The game is no longer consistent with a contemporary way of life. At its core, the game is about big, wide open, pastoral spaces and endless hours that one might idle away watching this game that was clearly created before television. Jackie Robinson had to "break the color line" in order to play the game. This was at a time when Black people needed to *prove* that they were worthy of White attention and acceptance. Though many baseball lovers, even some who happen to be Black, will decry the fact that the game seems to have lost its appeal for younger generations of Blacks, this is a waste of time. Baseball has little to no appeal for young Black people because the game is stuck in another era.

Not only is the game too slow, but it in no way speaks to the urban realities of this present generation. There are now large segments of the Black population that no longer feel the need to prove themselves to anyone. Baseball is too tied to its tradition, and this conservative posture is such that it is too confining for those who constitute the hip hop generation. The regressive history of baseball is something that has no appeal to those who have come up in the aftermath of the at times fawning posture of the civil rights movement, which was all about being accepted into the corridors of mainstream Whiteness. Though many of the best baseball players still happen to be Black, the number of good Black players decreases substantially as we move into the younger generation.

Football is more appealing than baseball for young African Americans, but it too has seen its best days. American football, as they call it in the rest of the "football"-playing world, was a sport that reached its zenith during the Cold War. The sport is imbued with a great deal of military imagery, again courtesy of its heyday in the heightened buildup of Cold War America. The emphasis on things like formations, field generals, and the strategic execution of various plays is directly rooted in this Cold War sensibility. Further, the game, like baseball, requires wide open spaces and again is not so well suited to the realities of the urban condition. Again, like baseball, the sport requires a relatively large number of participants.

Though football still attracts large numbers of spectators, the game is no longer responsive to the conditions of urban America. This is indicated in a most emphatic way when you consider that Los Angeles, the nation's second-largest city, has not had a professional football team since the mid-1990s. Consider that the Los Angeles Lakers are one of the most popular and most successful teams in professional sports. In this regard they assume a great deal of significance in the city's sense of cultural identity. The Lakers are now as much a part of LA's identity as Hollywood is. This can be read as an indication that those who live in the city feel no need for the distraction of a football team.

It is also important to point out that both baseball and football are almost uniquely American in their appeal and in their cultural representation. Baseball has of late featured some prominent Japanese players. This can be tied directly to America's imposition of its will on Japan in the post–World War II era. Other than that, the only other baseball players who come from places other than America in significant numbers tend to be from the Dominican Republic. This Caribbean nation too has become a fertile source for the development of baseball players. This situation then is just another example of American cultural imperialism relative to baseball, and not an indication of any worldwide appeal. Major league baseball has turned the Dominican Republic into its own farm system.

Taking this argument further, football is often referred to as "American football" throughout the rest of the *futbol*-playing world. When most people outside of America refer to football they are, of course, referring to the game known in America as "soccer." Therefore American football is almost exclusively American, and it in no way has any appeal outside of America. In keeping with the military emphasis and its Cold War sensibility, American football is especially xenophobic in the way that it assumes an almost exclusively American disposition.

Basketball, though, is a game uniquely suited to the urban environment. First of all, it requires very little space, and the space that it does require can often be found in public parks or community gyms. The equipment needed is minimal also. The game of basketball can also be played by an individual, unlike baseball or football, which require more people. In order to play baseball properly, you need baseball bats, balls, and gloves. To avoid injury in football, one needs the proper pads. Basketball can rely on public space, which tends to be available in urban areas, and it can be performed by a team of one.

It is these minimal requirements and the solitary pursuit that makes the game, at least in its initial stages, perfectly suited to the conditions of the inner city. This is not to say that great basketball players come only from the city. A statement like this would be absurd. Both Michael Jordan and Allen Iverson, for instance, hail from small Southern towns. What I am saying here is that even though the game has an appeal beyond its urban core, those who choose to play it, if they are to be successful, tend to adopt a particularly urban style and sensibility. This urban style and sensibility though are often in stark contrast to what is desired as the preferred mode of being. Though a relic like John Stockton of the Utah Jazz, who, for instance, refuses to wear the longer basketball shorts though they are now the norm, still draws a great deal of praise from many old-school figures, he and his kind are out of step with the changes that this urban hip hop aesthetic has brought to the game.

Basketball is also the sport, next to soccer, that has best recognized the changes going on in the global culture in which we now live. The NBA features players from all over the globe who have adopted the game, and other nations now routinely send quality players to the American professional league. In a world where nationalism seems to have given way to culture as a form of identity, basketball has become a culture of its own. This culture transcends America's shores, and in this world made smaller and potentially more accessible by virtue of technology, people from all over the globe both watch and participate. Baseball and football are ultimately local, whereas basketball is internationally known, nationally recognized, and locally accepted.

The soul of basketball, however, remains at least for the time being rooted in urban America. There is something potentially liberating that is inherent in the game as performed under this urban hip hop aegis. The game speaks in conjunction with and response to the conditions of urban America in a most direct way. In this regard, the game is connected to other forms of cultural expression that work to define and represent Black people as their contemporary selves. This is certainly true with regard to music.

Basketball and various forms of Black music have always had a strong point of connection. These are two arenas where Black people have had the best opportunity to express themselves, and where there continues to be a critical mass of individuals who use the opportunity to influence the culture at large and, hopefully, make some money in the process. These are two rarefied spaces where the most fundamental elements of Blackness are articulated and played out, both internally and for the masses.

In terms of contemporary society, as the Iverson situation demonstrates in no uncertain terms, of all the forms of cultural expression available to Black people, basketball has been most closely connected to the culture of hip hop. This unique relationship has evolved over time and is fueled by the social and economic conditions that have specifically beset Black urban communities since the dawn of the Reagan era in the early '80s. In my mind there is a singularity of purpose here that provides for this close connection. As a sport, basketball is again something that can be pursued by an individual. Individuals can perfect their own skills in solitude before going on to perform with a larger group of people.

Hip hop is the same way, in that rappers must first develop their lyrics in their own mind. This act of individual creativity takes place before there is any larger group participation. The Zenlike connection between rappers and their rhymes is at the core of hip hop's spiritual quest to properly define oneself. As Nas says, "All I need is one mic." This is very much like the oneness created between the basketball player and the game itself.

The two distinct entities connect so well because they deal with lack as opposed to excess. In the same way that basketball requires little space and requires few people, hip hop requires no instruments nor any formal music education or training. Rappers create rhymes and articulate them through their "mouthpiece," and this forms the basis of the relationship.

The other salient point here is that both basketball and hip hop offer unique opportunities for wealth and social mobility. This is unlike other walks of life, where the often invisible tenets of racism potentially hinder Black participation, especially for those Black people who hail from the lowest rung of the urban social ladder. Basketball and hip hop are based on one's ability to perform a specified artistic feat. Thus the two are not so subject to the whims and dictates of some abstract unwritten rules. In other words, success in these areas is based on merit instead of some ephemeral notion of having qualified for inclusion.

Recognizing this, basketball and hip hop are a marriage made in the upper room of American popular culture. The two go together like Mel Gibson and Danny Glover. To the extent that Black culture in general has always been the avant-garde of American culture—though never recognized as such—this unique merger of these two forms stands at the forefront of all that is hip, cutting edge, and controversial in contemporary American society.

Back in the day, Miles Davis, who was fascinated by the sweet science of boxing, would arrange his trumpet solos with the imagery of a Sugar Ray Robinson prizefight in mind. The poet laureate of soul, Marvin Gaye, wanted to play football, and he at one point had a tryout with the Detroit Lions. His close friendship with several of the team's stars, Lem Barney, Charlie Sanders, and Mel Farr, was such that these are the voices you hear chattering, talkin' shit, and providing background ambience on one of the most significant tunes ever recorded, the classic "What's Going On."

The seeds of these cross-cultural connections between sports and music have been planted for some time. Yet instead of boxing and jazz or soul and football, we now have basketball and hip hop, which changes the game, as it were, so as to accommodate our current imagination.

Real Recognize Real

Black culture has always been positioned between the poles of fear and entertainment in its relationship to the White mainstream. Various elements of White society have often tried to censor Black culture because it was thought to threaten a particular way of life. On the other hand, Black culture has at times been regarded as the most entertaining by those Whites who recognize the financial potential in it, or by those who see it as the epitome of hip and cool. Either way, it points to the fact that we tend to talk about Black culture as if it's always being performed for a White audience.

Most often our understanding of these two Black cultural forces is filtered through a White prism. The media and the sportscasters who comment on basketball are overwhelmingly White, and though there are some noted hip hop magazines, the image of hip hop in the public imagination is one that is controlled by a dominant White gaze also.

This is a situation where perceptions about Black culture tend to override what the culture might have to say about itself. The mainstream often pigeonholes Black culture, forcing the culture to accommodate whatever perceptions might already be in place as opposed to allowing it to exist on its own terms and give off its own representation.

Basketball and hip hop, however, do serve as contemporary examples of these contradictions. The two function like a stage, providing us with a melodramatic racial theater where the most compelling ghetto drama unfolds far beyond the actual site of the performance itself. Today, basketball and hip hop also happen to occupy two unique spaces in American society, where the issues are based on a Black norm as opposed to a White standard, as is usually the case.

Are the connotations the same when the audience is different? Is it even possible to move away from the preeminence of the White gaze in our thinking about these issues in the first place?

Far from being simply music played on one's headphones that is then unconsciously imitated by those who listen, hip hop is the sound-track to a lifestyle; and basketball tends to be the most visible stage where this lifestyle is played out. There is potentially a different per-spective when we look at the worlds of basketball and hip hop from the vantage point of the culture itself. As the rapper Method Man has asked rhetorically, "Who the fuck wanna die for they culture?"—here sug-gesting the seriousness with which the culture is regarded. An under-standing of the individuals and their culture along with the cultural references themselves that inform their generation is required knowl-edge if we are to break away from this dominant White interpretation.

How do we begin to understand the culture on its own terms? First of all, considering that basketball and hip hop have consistently pro-vided tangible economic opportunities for young Black men, many re-gard these to be the only viable options in a society where many other opportunities continue to be closed off. With this sense of social mo-bility at its core, 'ball and hip hop redefine the American dream from the perspective of the young, Black, and famous.

As the most recent NBA trends indicate, the future of the league will rely on the development of several millionaire teenagers who have gone straight from high school to the pros, and in the process straight from "ashy to classy" in Biggie Smalls' words, from being mired in poverty to wallowing in wealth. Many critics suggest that it is inappropriate for these uneducated Black "thugs" to make so much money, especially now that they are routinely eschewing college to get a jump start on earn-ing their millions. Yet in a sport like tennis, for instance, which in spite of Venus and Serena Williams' current success and prominence is still perceived to be a White, upper-middle-class sport, there is no call for the imposition of a player age limit like the one being proposed by NBA commissioner David Stern and supported by many others.

Is this the classic racial double standard at work? Why does this racial cloud of negative perception loom over young Black men who have money? Is this possibility a real threat to society?

Previous generations of African Americans were thought to have to "sell out," to assimilate, in order to make it in mainstream society. Yet this hip hop generation has decided that though they want the money and power offered by mainstream society, they do not want to have to change in order to get it. They want to be *of* the mainstream without being *in* the mainstream.

Can people in the mainstream accept the fact that there are those who want what they have to offer, but who want no part of what they are about?

The large sums of money generated by 'ball and hip hop produce a certain freedom and independence among those young Black men who have it; and it can also produce a certain disregard for the racial constraints that are often imposed upon or expected of them.

This book will discuss how both forms of culture have gone from being dismissed, reviled, and rejected by the mainstream to being embraced, indulged, and imitated. In the late '70s, pro basketball was thought to be a league of overpaid Black drug addicts, and it consequently commanded little public or media attention. This is the same time that hip hop was emerging from the boroughs of New York and becoming the rage throughout ghettos all over America while simultaneously becoming the scourge of society for many others.

Though the connection between basketball and hip hop was less evident at first, the seeds of the connection have always been there. Many may remember pioneering rapper Kurtis Blow and his novelty hit "Basketball" from the mid-'80s as an early example of the connection as expressed through the music itself. "Basketball is my favorite sport / I like the way they dribble / up and down the court / Just like I'm the King on the microphone / so is Dr. J and Moses Malone." In the song, Blow makes a direct link between his prowess as an MC and the abilities of the game's most compelling performers. He goes on to rap about his love for all facets of the game and extols the virtues of many of that era's best players. Yet it did take some time before this connection between basketball and hip hop was firmly established and identifiable to the public at large.

Throughout the 1980s, basketball pursued a course of mainstream acceptance highlighted by the Magic/Bird, Black/White, East Coast/ West Coast rivalry that began the decade. By the late '80s/early '90s a new generation of players came into the league who had grown up with hip hop as their own soundtrack, and as the music itself started to emerge in the culture, its connection to basketball became increasingly visible. Now, some thirty-plus years later, the NBA represents one of the most recognizable cultural brand names in the world, and hip hop has made its mark as a distinct global commodity and cultural force as well. Over time the connection between basketball and hip hop would evolve and become increasingly more evident. It is important then to follow this journey if we are to fully appreciate the present moment.

Basketball has been represented in other areas of popular culture also. Films like *White Men Can't Jump* and *Hoop Dreams*, or the television cult classic *The White Shadow*, which featured a predominantly Black inner-city Los Angeles high school basketball team coached by a former White NBA player, represented the game as a unique symbol of urban culture. Basketball is also in constant conversation with Black popular culture at a larger level in that the images coming from the game tend to affirm or counteract other representations of Blackness at any given time. But it is the present synthesis of basketball and hip hop that most effectively reflects the unique expression of urban Black men from a particular generation, and that in all its manifestations underlies the forward movement of the young, Black, rich and famous.

LeBron James, high school phenom-turned-NBA-multi-millionaire, the man known as "King James" to the masses, is without a doubt the latest embodiment of the sentiments expressed in this book. James as a high school player drew more attention than many NBA players during the 2002–03 season. Some of his high school games were broadcast to a national audience on ESPN2. To some he was controversial, to others a hero, another example of a hip hop baller who'd emerged from the worst living conditions to reap fame and fortune at a very young age. By the summer of 2003, James had truly become The King, signing a $90 million endorsement deal with Nike, double the amount given to established NBA superstar Kobe Bryant, and inking a huge deal with Upper Deck Trading Cards. At the 2003 NBA draft, he was the number one pick of the Cleveland Cavaliers, the team he had grown up watching from his nearby home in Akron, Ohio. He strolled up to the stage dressed in white from head to toe, suited and booted, clean as a cooked chitlin'. This was the King's coronation. Only time will tell what becomes of King James, but he promises to fulfill the obligations of the young, Black, rich and famous for many years to come.

Don't Get High on Your Own Supply
The NBA's Image Problem Back in the Day

Flying high in the friendly sky /
Without ever leaving the ground.

—MARVIN GAYE
"Flying High in the Friendly Sky"

AM I BLACK ENOUGH FOR YOU?

n order to understand the significance of basketball as the vehicle for the expression of larger urban issues, especially its connection to hip hop culture in the present, we must first go back to a time before these connections were clear and place the sport itself in its proper 1970s context. There is no question now that the '70s served as the watershed point for the mainstream emergence of Black popular culture. As a direct result of both the civil rights and the Black Power movements' impact on the American imagination, Black popular culture began to be visible, if not cutting edge, across a broad spectrum that included film, television, music, and sports, and in this regard basketball would become a central component in helping to define the changing definition of Black America.

The Blaxploitation era in Hollywood, which produced films like *Shaft, Superfly,* and *The Mack,* highlighted the essence of supercool. This was consistent with the popular Black situation comedies on television featuring a memorable cast of characters that included: Fred Sanford, J. J. Evans, George and Weezy Jefferson. In addition there was also the lasting influence of shows like *Fat Albert* and *Soul Train*. In the recording studios, artists like Marvin Gaye, Aretha Franklin, Curtis Mayfield, and George Clinton were redefining the idea of Black music. And of course, on the playing fields of the sporting life, Hank Aaron was breaking records, O. J. Simpson was breaking tackles, and Muhammad Ali was breaking it all down. Black culture was at once hip, prominent, and substantial. No longer confined to the Jim Crow car of underground racial existence, Black culture was everywhere, all at once.

The growing number of Black entertainers, a sizable number compared to before the '70s, formed a unique celebrity class. As this culture moment began to bloom, it became evident that members of this group were as glamorous, if not more so, than their White counterparts. Prominently featured in *Ebony* and *Jet* magazines at a time when these publications were still relevant, the new class of Black celebrity was now also getting mainstream attention as well with regular coverage in places like *TV Guide* and *Time*, among others.

Their numbers were increasing, and along with this their bankrolls were getting larger. Long the darlings of a Black world deprived of mainstream recognition, now the Black celebrity class had become the epitome of what was thought to be cool by White audiences eager to sink their teeth into the hip new thing. The blacker the berry, the sweeter the juice, indeed!

That Nigger's Crazy

The person most indicative of this newly visible type of transcendent Black culture came in the comedic form of Richard Pryor. Born in the working-class hell of Peoria, Illinois, Pryor skated through the '60s as a Bill Cosby imitator, dulling his own style so as to get in where he fit in, that is, as a subordinate to Cosby's nonthreatening, affable image. Of course, there was room for only one Black style at a time, so Pryor made it easy on himself and simply offered his own lower-rent version of

Cosby's accepted act. Yet, as the '60s gave way to the '70s, Pryor became bored and wanted to shake loose from his confinement to these tired conventions.

As legend would have it, Pryor appeared on a Las Vegas stage one night in the late '60s and, realizing that he was lost in a haze of self-delusion, trying to be something he was not, he posed a rhetorical question to himself, "What the fuck am I doing here?" Shortly thereafter, frustrated at what he had become, he jumped in a car, bolted back to Los Angeles, and eventually made his way up to Northern California, leaving behind the comedy world in which he had so desperately tried to fit in.

While in the Bay Area, Pryor began hanging out with a group of Black writers, artists, and revolutionary figures that included Cecil Brown, author of *The Lives and Loves of a Jiveass Nigger*, Ishmael Reed, author of numerous tomes including *Mumbo Jumbo*, and even Huey P. Newton—the revolutionary parading as a folk hero—who was responsible for putting the Black Panther Party for Self-Defense front and center in the contentious debates around the evolving function of race in America. After this revolutionary baptism by fire, Pryor came to consciousness, as they say, and his comedy would be deeply politicized from there on out. No longer was he a Cosby clone. Instead he became the very antithesis of Cosby's palpably nonthreatening persona. Pryor, who had left the stage a "negro," emerged from this consciousness-raising experience a "nigger." Embracing the street sensibility of Black masculinity and putting it in a politically contextualized form, Pryor went on to become the hottest comic—period, Black or White—by the mid-'70s.

Having made a string of records on the underground Laugh Records label, Pryor, by 1974, was recording his comedy on the mega Warner Brothers label and not compromising one bit because of it. His album *That Nigger's Crazy* (1974) stands out as one of the most important comedy records and social statements ever made on wax. Pryor went on to achieve unparalleled success and significance with a string of albums including *Is It Something I Said?* (1975), *Bicentennial Nigger* (1976), and his most accomplished work, *Wanted: Live in Concert* (1978).

Through these albums, Pryor's stream of consciousness moved between Black folk culture, Black nationalism, and his own personal tribulations to establish a truly incredible body of work that would be imitated for years to come. Pryor's work here was similar to what Marvin Gaye had done on his monumental album *What's Going On* some years before. Pryor's discussion of race relations still stands as one of the most honest assessments of such matters ever heard in the vein of popular culture.

Pryor was also quite successful beyond his comedy albums. With his appearances in several films of the era, such as *The Mack* (1973), *Uptown Saturday Night* (1974), and *Car Wash* (1976), he steals the show. In Paul Schrader's *Blue Collar* (1978), Pryor demonstrates some impressive dramatic chops as well. Pryor was so popular that NBC wanted him to be the inaugural host of their comedy show *Saturday Night Live* in 1975. But they were so concerned about his potential use of unacceptable language on a live program that they postponed his appearance for a few weeks, and then broadcast the show on a five-second delay so as to allow network censors to bleep out anything potentially problematic. He also hosted his own short-lived variety show, which was eventually canceled by the NBC network over "creative differences." Pryor could never be made to fit the straitjacketed world of network television.

The point here is this: Richard Pryor was a major star of the 1970s. A Black star who had come to mainstream prominence doing decidedly Black comedy, material that often went against the grain of what was accepted discourse on topics like race relations, sex, and drug use. He was a countercultural antihero for some, and a real Black man for others. He was bigger than US Steel. He was also a dope fiend.

In early '80s, Pryor doused himself with some cognac and lit himself on fire in what he later revealed was a suicide attempt. Fame and fortune had created a monster, one that could not run away from those Peoria demons that haunted him. He had grown up in a "hoe house," with his grandmother serving as the madam and his own mother working the night shift. The vivid memories of that time would serve well as material in his comedy act, and would also serve to tear away at his soul. Pryor's mad dash through the streets of the San Fernando Valley after setting himself on fire was as much a cry for help as it was a clear indicator of his own self-destructive behavior.

What was more striking here though was that this drug-induced sprint had been fueled by the cocaine paranoia that came not from snorting the drug—as was commonplace at that time in Hollywood—but from "freebasing" it. Yes, Richard Pryor exposed the square world to the art of smoking the pipe. Not content with the normal high that came from ingesting the white powder through his nose, Pryor and others on the hip, cutting edge of the drug underworld would boil the impurities out of the drug using ether and then, using a blowtorch, inhale smoke from the cocaine lava rocks that had formed in this cooking process. The high was more intense than snorting but it lasted for a much shorter time, thus the user needed more cocaine to reach his case. Pryor, a pyromaniac of the self, not only foregrounded his self-destructive urges, but also revealed what was going on in the rarefied spaces of this newly defined Black celebrity lifestyle. This was at once sad and potentially glamorous.

Pryor's search for the ultimate high was a Dionysian pursuit that extolled the virtues of a journey through Huxley's doors of perception and an indicator of what the idle rich often do with their time and money. Most everyday people had not even been exposed to cocaine at this point, much less freebasing. No, cocaine was a drug for the beautiful people, the wealthy, the stars, the glamorous ones for whom money and access were no object. Freebasing was the next level, and beyond.

———

MY CONCERN HERE is less about why Pryor tried to destroy himself and more about the fact that he did. To see him now, confined to a wheelchair, unable to speak, is like looking at a once-vicious cobra that has been defanged. Both Pryor and Muhammad Ali make us ask the question, who really got the last laugh?

These individuals were once strong, bold Black men who did not bite their tongue, especially when it came to telling it like it was about racism and White supremacy as it existed in America. Now, sadly, they are silent, helpless victims, weak, frail mascots who are publicly paraded around so as to confirm and document their muted march toward death. America has the last laugh.

At one time though, Richard Pryor was THE MAN. Far from being a helpless victim, he articulated a supreme indifference to the codes of acceptable behavior prescribed for so many Black men before him. He took chances. He bucked tradition. He was a nigger and proud of it. His cocaine use only served to underscore his supreme indifference. Not only did he not "give a fuck," as it were, but the dope usage also allowed him to exist in his own world, where he did not have to give a fuck. The cocaine helped buffer him from the slings and arrows of a White populace that served up equal parts of love and hate; love for his unabashed talents and hate for his use of this talent in critiquing their own racism.

Pryor, like so many others, used the cocaine to form an invisible white circle around himself. Yet at some point he became a prisoner in that very circle. The cocaine fueled his comedy, it exemplified his anger, and it ultimately precipitated his downfall.

Yet in all of this, he was a star, a glamorous star whose pathologies were played out for the same public that bent over laughing at his jokes. He was equal parts rebel, icon, role model for dope fiends, and martyr. Pryor typified the difficulties of Black success in a still-hostile White America. And he was certainly not alone.

In the end Richard Pryor self-destructed, though his "I don't give a fuck" attitude was certainly a precursor to and for the hip hop generation that grew up in his shadow. This new generation would witness the slow destruction of many around them due to crack cocaine. So many of them decided that instead of destroying themselves, they would turn this same attitude of supreme indifference into a weapon against their detractors and use this distinct form of cultural identity as a viable commercial force.

Basketball Jones

In the summer of 1980, Chris Cobbs, a writer for the *Los Angeles Times*, penned a revelatory piece entitled "NBA and Cocaine: Nothing to Snort At," on the way in which the drug cocaine had come to infiltrate the

National Basketball Association (NBA). Cobbs' influential piece would be accepted and referenced by many of that time as an indication that the NBA was out of control. The piece, which relies on many unnamed sources, suggested that possibly as many as 75 percent of the league's players were regular cocaine users. It went on to hint that at least 10 percent of those using cocaine indulged in a derivative form of smoking cocaine made famous by Richard Pryor and known as freebasing. Cobbs also points out in the article that Black players at that time made up more than 70 percent of the NBA's personnel. In other words, this predominantly Black league, reflecting widely held perceptions about the Black population at large, had a drug problem.

———

UNLIKE BASEBALL OR FOOTBALL, the two most popular sports of that time, basketball was not only made up of a majority of Black players, but it was, more important, beginning to be perceived as *Black*. Basketball as a sport was still relatively low key in the late '70s/early '80s. Baseball was the national pastime and football was the most popular spectator sport. Basketball, particularly pro basketball, could claim only a handful of loyal aficionados. It did not help that the sport had such an overwhelmingly Black presence.

Baseball and football are very regimented. A player assumes a certain position and then is expected to play that position. If all the players play their positions properly, then it is assumed that the team will be successful. Each of these positions is highly specialized and many of them are often in use at separate times. A pitcher in baseball is not expected to be a great hitter. And a quarterback in football is not expected to make any tackles. They do their respective jobs and leave it at that.

Basketball is different. During the '70s things were a bit more regimented than now, but centers would on occasion be expected to shoot, forwards might have to dribble the basketball, and a guard could be required to grab a rebound. In other words, the players are all on the floor at the same time and thus they all might be expected to periodically do something outside of what the job description of their position requires. Basketball players were less specialists than in the other sports. They were *athletes*, and this has become increasingly the case through the present day.

In addition, compared to the rigidity with which the other sports enforced the task of playing one's position, basketball offered a more free-flowing experience. It was more open, more liberal by its very nature. Or at least it possessed the possibility of a certain liberation in the way that it was performed. This intensified as Black players came to dominate the league.

To some extent, I am arguing here that basketball would, over time, come to be the sport of choice as Black players, and by extension Black people, moved deeper and deeper into the fabric of everyday American life. Jackie Robinson had to prove himself, and prove to America, that a Black athlete was worthy of playing the national pastime. This was very much like boxer Joe Louis and Olympic track star Jesse Owens demonstrating to America and the world at large with their groundbreaking athletic triumphs in the 1930s that Black athletes were now essential in defining America's image.

As stated previously, football, the unique American version, that is, with all its masculine overtures and militaristic metaphors, had come to prominence during the Cold War. The Cold War imposed a sense of regimentation on the country at large. In connection with this, Black football players served a role. But that role was ultimately confined to a singular importance. One was part of a team, a team led by the coach, modeled in the image of General Patton. In other words, you were expected to be a soldier, and soldiers follow orders. Considering this strict code of military conduct, there was no room for renegades.

What I am suggesting here is that baseball and football were already predetermined to be extensions of the American blue-collar ethos and, at some point, the Cold War ethic. Individuality was subsumed, contained, in the name of group productivity. This was the White American way of life writ large, and Blacks need only be concerned to the extent that they were useful, which increasingly became the case as time passed. I am not suggesting that there were no stars of this era, but I am suggesting that the stars themselves were embraced, even coddled, by the tradition and ultimately were cogs in a much larger machine.

Basketball was different. Since America already had a pastime in baseball and in football a larger-than-life spectator sport, there was really no need for any other sport. This was especially true in an era when television had yet to fully utilize sports as a staple of its programming. Basketball was able to develop in relative obscurity, without the burden of being either a pastime or really popular, for that matter. The sport was able to come in under the radar of the American public.

This again adds a level of inherent flexibility to the way that sport functioned. In other words, there was no need to break any color barriers when no one was paying attention anyway. While certainly American and indebted to the American way of life, basketball was free to develop into whatever it would become without the added burden of having to conform to the larger ideal, though this demand was never completely absent from the equation at some level.

As a matter of fact, the most popular basketball players throughout most of the twentieth century had been the Harlem Globetrotters, Abe Saperstein's barnstorming Black team that combined equal parts "Uncle Tomming" with a spectacular and unparalleled display of basketball skills. America, to the extent that it had any consciousness of basketball, knew the Globetrotters and had come to accept their brand of minstrel basketball as authentic. Basketball then was already perceived to be more entertainment than sport.

By the late '70s/early '80s, television had found sports to be a steady revenue stream and basketball, though still relatively obscure on television, was starting to gain some visibility and would garner more and more as the television cameras focused their attention. The game was, as previously stated, different in its orientation.

Again, unlike football and baseball, basketball required only a handful of players. Teams consisted of twelve players, and only five of them could play at a time. Baseball and football, respectively, featured as many players on the field at one time as the total number of basketball players on a given team. The impact that one player could have was substantially increased on a basketball team.

In football, for instance, a team might want to build a strong running game. In order to do so they would need not only a great tailback, but also a solid offensive line, as one great tailback against eleven defenders is a recipe for failure and possibly career-ending injury. In other words, you need at least six people, maybe seven, including a good blocking back, in order to establish a strong running game. In essence, a football team must build its running game one player at a time.

In basketball, though, you can change the course of a team's fortunes by simply adding one excellent player. The Chicago Bulls went from NBA doormat to being arguably the greatest team in the game to date by drafting Michael Jordan. Sure, they had to build a nucleus of role players around him, but Jordan's ability to dominate both ends of the court at will nullified the need to build brick-by-brick. The same could be said of Magic Johnson, Larry Bird, Julius Erving, and Shaquille O'Neal, among others, all individual players whose singular presence immediately turned their subpar or underachieving teams into title contenders.

This being the case, basketball is again revealed to be a sport more akin to entertainment. The cult of the superstar is already embedded in the game's possibilities. At the end of the day, one superstar, who demands a large salary and commands much attention, can be the catalyst to earning huge profits for the owners. Basketball is here more like Hollywood. It is a star culture, a celebrity-centered entertainment venue and ultimately more suited to the concept than either baseball or football could ever hope to be.

Yet by the same token it is a sport; and for this reason people will always want to apply the same criteria to basketball that they do to all other sports, regardless of these special circumstances. When you add the facts that the majority of basketball players are Black, that most of America's thinking about sport developed at a different time in history, and that this influential Black cultural style has had a massive impact on the game's overall perception, then you have a truly unique sport, and one that cannot be judged in the way that sports have been in the past.

Jazz and 'Ball

If we apply this entertainment model to basketball, or at least one somewhere between entertainment and sport, then it is possible to understand why the game was facing these allegations of cocaine abuse in the early '80s. To begin with, basketball players to me tend to be like great artists, and at that time they were very much like the legendary jazz musicians. The game they toiled in, 'ball, was less grunt work, less yeomanlike drudgery, though it undoubtedly contained aspects of this. Instead, the game was about finesse and style. When done properly the game was performed with the same passion that John Coltrane had articulated on the bandstand, or, on the other end, the game often looked like it was being played with the same ease that Lester Young exhibited when doing his thing.

Though many people might make an allusion to a perceived connection between basketball and jazz, to me there are two very real links that unite them. These are the idea of improvisation and the visibility of a critical mass of Black bodies. You need one in order to truly understand the other.

What has always distinguished jazz from, say, classical music is this notion of improvisation. Classical music has always been about a certain replication of the original. A classical musician is given the charge of performing a piece of music in as close a proximity to the original text as possible, with few mistakes and less room for interpretation. The original is invested with ultimate authority, and anything else is perceived to be secondary if not inferior to the original.

Jazz on the other hand is about improvisation. The original exists as a reference point, but in no way is it the sole embodiment of all authority. As a matter of fact, to imitate the original is to "bite" or copy, and this is deemed to be repetition and definitely unoriginal in its approach. This is frowned upon. Jazz musicians are given credit when they create, when they interpret, when they strike out on their own and make their own original statements.

For many years basketball was performed in the manner of classical music. A player was supposed to follow what was called textbook style, and not deviate in the process. Showmanship was discouraged. The game was to be played according to the dictates set down before it or else it was thought it would dissolve into chaos. Yet, as many Black players from the inner city came to dominate the game, this textbook style began to be challenged. The style of the playground reigned, and a more athletic style of play—which assisted in the improvisation—was what made you significant. Your ability to create and do so with flair was what made the crowds gasp, not some adherence to an elusive and outdated textbook. This was similar to a jazz musician playing his instrument with a style all his own. Imitation would get you derisively dismissed, while originality would separate you from the pack.

———

BASKETBALL IN THE '70S was fighting a style war, with the textbook style of old being challenged by the growing influence of the new, more wide open playground style. When the American Basketball Association (ABA) was collapsed into the NBA, bringing with it a number of players known for doing their own thing, the league would become engaged in a battle over which style and ultimately which philosophy would prevail.

It is here that this issue of critical mass becomes significant. As more and more Black athletes were admitted to major university basketball programs in the '60s, and in turn more and more Black players came into the professional game in the '70s, the style of the game itself started to shift. Traditionalists would often cry foul. Regardless, the game was being transformed before our very eyes. This was not only indicative of the stylistic differences though, it was indicative of a fundamental cultural shift as well.

Basketball was becoming a *Black* sport, and not just in numbers but also in overall vibe and attitude. No longer would Black players subsume their flash and unique expression for the glory of playing the game the *right* way. Now they would increasingly demand the right to play the game in a manner consistent with their formative years. This new breed of player had learned the game in that highly competitive conservatory known as the playground.

Contrary to popular belief, the creativity and showmanship of the playground were not a rejection of the concepts of winning or of not placing the individual above and beyond the team, however vocally detractors might argue the point. This streetball style was about making an increasingly Black game respond to the latest developments taking place on the playground blacktop instead of it being some museum piece, put under glass and left to die an unnatural death.

Players were evaluated not only on ability but also on how good they looked when playing. Style was very important; one had to look the part as well as act it. This again was altogether different from the puritanlike, blue-collar antistyle that had dominated much of the sport before the emergence of this Black critical mass. These new style arbiters who came out in the 1970s—a period that would become basketball's point of modern transition—all possessed something special, a trick, a treat, something that made them stand out as artists. With Dr. J it was his extended right arm, ball palmed just so. For Kareem Abdul-Jabbar it was his automatic "sky hook." David Thompson invented "skywalking," and "The Iceman" George Gervin patented the "finger roll." As the Iceman himself said in a famous retro Nike commercial from the early '90s, "One thing I could do, was finger roll."

These individuals were the first generation to inherit what had become a *Black* game. As many of America's universities, especially those in the South, started opening up to Black athletes in the late '60s, the game of basketball started to change. In many cases the Black athletes were the largest bloc of Black students attending certain colleges in any visible numbers.

The players had been uprooted from their communities and placed in an alien culture, but given the opportunity to perform. This transition could not have been easy. The players in question were really like hired hands, what in Germany are called Gastarbeiters, or guest workers, who are given an opportunity to work, in this case play, but are offered no other citizenship rights. They were and are, in a sense, athletic mercenaries.

Though there had been Black players in the game before, the changing culture at the collegiate level created something new, a critical mass of Black bodies interested in and highly capable of playing basketball for a living. College basketball was for them like a premed or prelaw program, an opportunity to make a living in the future without having to work as some blue-collar slave or hustle their way through the mean streets of urban America. Playing 'ball also allowed them to do something with a certain style intact.

There was such a pool of talent to choose from that at one point there were two separate professional leagues: the NBA and the American Basketball Association (ABA). The ABA began competing with the NBA for the best college players, and they allowed for a more liberal style of basketball. The game played on the ABA courts was more akin to the game as it was performed on the playgrounds of urban America. It was a game based more on athleticism, style, and creativity. And this is where the improvisation comes in. Basketball in the ABA would function more like jazz music, breaking away from the more classical-minded textbook version of the staid NBA. By the '70s the NBA was forced to change also.

The ABA started stealing the best college players from the NBA, and even exceptional high school players like Moses Malone made the leap. The NBA had to realize that though they were the more traditional of the two leagues, and had a more solid financial footing, the best players were playing the best basketball somewhere else. The NBA may have had the textbook tradition of the Boston Celtics, but everyone knew that Julius Erving was the best and most exciting player in the game, even though he was playing in the lesser of the two leagues.

In 1976 the ABA went out of business, with its remaining four teams—Denver Nuggets, New Jersey Nets, San Antonio Spurs, and Indiana Pacers—merging into the NBA. The real prize of this merger though was the fact that the NBA was now the only game in town and no longer had to compete for the best talent. It was now guaranteed all the best, most exciting, and defiantly cutting-edge players were available.

This being the case, the NBA had now also made an unwritten pact with the culture of streetball that would forever change the landscape of the game. This new generation of basketball players was not so easily contained by the strict rules of a more traditional NBA. No, they were self-assured, glamorous, if not a bit militant in their approach. They had cut their teeth on the defiant aura of the Black Panthers, around the free spirit of funk musician George Clinton, and in the mold of the greatest himself, Muhammad Ali. They were Black athletes, but they were Black men first, and the NBA had to, in some way or another, reconcile all of this with their incredible basketball skills.

The best of these new superstars of the game were artists as much as athletes. They were not these blue-collar working stiffs that baseball and football had provided for the masses. No, these basketball players demanded the attention of any great artist, fully expecting that they would be treated accordingly.

The new breed had risen up from the ashes of America's worst ghettos and rural Southern towns and had come to make a living performing for large White audiences. This was not work, it was passion, and more important, it was play. Yet it was also a life-support system, offering one of the few opportunities in this society for a Black man to make a living for himself and his extended family, and to do so while being cool at the same time.

Spencer for Hire

Yes. We were converts to the Church of Cocaine.
We were the high priests of Cool. Hallelujah.
— SPENCER HAYWOOD
in *Spencer Haywood:*
The Rise, The Fall, The Recovery

The most interesting case study in this regard is the former player Spencer Haywood. In the early '70s, Haywood challenged the NBA's rules by signing early with the Seattle SuperSonics. The rule in question stipulated that a player's college class had to have graduated before that player could enter the league. Haywood argued that since he was the sole financial support for his entire family he should be able to begin earning a living regardless of the league's age requirement.

The Supreme Court eventually ruled in Haywood's favor, referring to the basketball player as a "hardship" case, with hardship here referring to economic hardship. With this gesture and phrasing, basketball would forever become a game where the politics of race and class would play a dominant part in its overall perception.

Haywood went on to have a distinguished career, though he jumped around the league, playing at different times for the Seattle Super-Sonics, the New York Knicks, the Los Angeles Lakers, and the Washington Bullets. At one point Haywood led a real life of luxury: big money, flashy cars, and NBA celebrity, all topped off by his marriage to one of the first Black supermodels, Iman.

Then it all came tumbling down. While participating in a stretching exercise during practice for the 1980 finals during his stint with the Lakers, Haywood fell asleep. After this sleep lapse, Haywood was suspended for the rest of the playoffs by interim Laker coach Paul Westhead. For those who did not already know, Haywood was using cocaine and had been up all night before indulging his love for the white powder, that "girl" as it was called in those days. While some might consider a Black player going to sleep during practice to be the worst example of a stereotype about "lazy shiftless niggers" that dates back at least to the days of Stepin Fetchit, I find Haywood's actions to be emblematic of a trend running through the league and the culture at large during that time.

Haywood was a dope fiend. Like Charlie Parker, Richard Pryor, and many others before him, and after him, Haywood's strength was also revealed to be his weakness. The same passion that made him a young superstar had now turned on him. Haywood, as in the oft-repeated phrase from the dope cult classic *Scarface* (1983), had begun to "get high on his own supply"; the supply here being both cocaine and his own ego.

Here was a guy who had a decade earlier presented an effective legal challenge to the league and prevailed. His case had made it possible for a legion of young Black men to get an early chance at fame, fortune, and wealth by trading in on their basketball skills; skills that White owners and White spectators were willing to pay to see put on display. Haywood's actions had given him and others like him the opportunity to live out the American Dream, a dream that someone like him had previously only experienced as a nightmare. Now, here he was ten years later, living out a nightmare of another sort. His fame, fortune, and wealth had led to unforeseen difficulties; mo' money, mo' problems, indeed.

What do you do when you go from rags to riches overnight? When you experience what rapper Biggie Smalls was talking about when he said he went from "ten keys of blow / to thirty G's a show / to orgies with hoes I never seen befoe." What happens when you have probably never had a checking account, and then you wake up one morning with a million dollars at your disposal? Though life in the ghetto may have taught you a great deal about handling adversity, it had probably taught you little about dealing with success.

The immense pressure of having to produce day in and day out, to be "on," as it were, all the time, to manage your money, to fend off greedy relatives, to avoid those wolves in sheep's clothing, to simply exist as a Black man in a still-hostile America was simply too much for someone trained only to play basketball. There were, I'm sure, no classes on life being offered where Spencer was enrolled. No. This would be too much for anyone to handle, much less a young urban Black man who hailed from the most impoverished of inner-city circumstances. In effect, Haywood, having at one time gone from rags to riches, had now gone from sugar to shit.

This is not an apology, though. It is an explanation. Haywood could break a defender down like he was nothing, but he could not break down the world. As a matter of fact, the weight of the world broke him down. Spencer Haywood was a casualty of the war America still continued to wage on its Black citizens, rich and poor. He was also his own worst enemy.

This is not to suggest that Haywood was alone in his "fuckups." He was, like many of his colleagues at the time, thought to be representative of the decline of the very league that he had once challenged. At various times other NBA players such as Bernard King, Michael Ray Richardson, John Lucas, Eddie Johnson, John Drew, Roy Tarpley, Richard Dumas, and David Thompson had been seduced by the same brilliant sparkle of a particular white girl. The indulgent actions of these players had come to dominate perceptions of the league itself, one now being not so subtly touted as a collection of overpaid, underachieving, selfish, arrogant niggers. In many cases the players were perceived as the equivalent of criminals, thought to be stealing money and attention from those more deserving White athletes or the most humble, and thus more easily controlled, Black ones.

TOO HIGH

Take the case of Denver Nuggets superstar David Thompson. "The Skywalker," as Thompson was known, hailed from a small town in rural North Carolina. This was in contrast to a player like Spencer Haywood, who had migrated from the South as a child and grown up in the decaying postindustrial urban oasis known as Detroit. These two examples suggest not only that basketball's impact on Black culture was both urban and rural, they demonstrate the far-flung power of the game as an opportunity for social and economic mobility.

Thompson had single-handedly stopped the seemingly invincible seven-year reign of UCLA atop college basketball while a player at North Carolina State in the early '70s. Thompson led NC State to the NCAA championship in 1973, beating UCLA in the Final Four. A few years later Thompson was battling the more popular Dr. J for the unspoken title of the best baller in the game. At that time Thompson played for the Denver Nuggets, who, along with Dr. J's New York Nets, were still playing in the struggling ABA.

The 1976 ABA All-Star Game featured a dunk contest between Dr. J and Thompson, which in my mind was the greatest dunk contest ever, even eclipsing the fabled Michael Jordan/Dominique Wilkins NBA rivalry that would develop in the late '80s. Dr. J won the dunk contest with a legendary jump from the free throw line. Thompson was a close second, actually leaving an incredible overall impression with his dunks. He was only six-foot-four, but he possessed an amazing forty-four-inch vertical leap along with the ability to hang suspended in the air for long periods of time. I would say that while Michael Jordan clearly drew a lot of his game from Dr. J, there was a great deal of David Thompson there also.

Thompson's career though was ultimately a big disappointment. He offered flashes of genius, as in that dunk contest performance, but never really lived up to his potential. Injuries and cocaine use short-circuited a promising start. In 1984 a high-flying Thompson fell down a flight of stairs at the famed New York nightclub Studio 54 and suffered injuries to his knee that effectively ended his career. This fall from grace was both tragic and ironic. What could be more indicative of a life of hedonism than a cocaine-induced fall at that palace of excess? Thompson, like several others, had gone out with a bang and would forever be relegated to the "shoulda, woulda, coulda" school of potential basketball achievement.

Hollywood and the world of rock and roll had often implied that there was a connection between the indulgent personalities of its superstars and their ability to perform, to produce artistry at the highest level. But not here. No, basketball would never be afforded this lofty status. Nor would it be accorded this sense of understanding. Basketball instead was dismissed as a waste of time, even by the television networks.

> *The players are so street-smart, their sophistication*
> *is just below that of a hardened convict.*
> *They know every angle on how to get women and drugs.*
> *They are so far ahead of the security men it's unbelievable.*
> *They know every hustle.*
> —ANONYMOUS SOURCE
> quoted in the *Los Angeles Times* article
> "NBA Cocaine: Nothing to Snort At"

Basketball, like other segments of American culture in the late '70s/early '80s, was being engulfed by this increasingly popular cocaine culture. Lots of money and loads of free time had created a space where this indulgence was starting to become commonplace. Yet, like the jazz musicians of the bebop and postbebop era, this culture of cocaine was about something other than just simple indulgence or garden-variety self-destruction.

Jazz musicians had often smoked "weed"—like Louis Armstrong did for most of his life—or in other cases they used heroin—that "boy" as it was called—to separate themselves from the masses, including the masses of other jazz musicians. The dope provided a buffer against the outside world, and it also created an insular culture of cool for those who used it, something akin to an exclusive VIP room for the truly initiated. Users formed their own clique, a secret society of sorts, and any nonuser was thought to be square and to some extent representative of the mainstream. This is just one of the ways that Black men have long attempted to exist in American society.

The use of indifference to the ways of the world historically had served Black men well, and the dope helped push this indifference to another level. With dope it could now be a supreme indifference that shouted loud and clear to all who would listen, "I really don't give a fuck." This indifference, this rejection of the standard mode of behavior, was a cause for concern though. The mainstream did not know what to do with individuals who did not buy into its philosophy, especially when they were Black figures who, the thinking went, should have been grateful for the opportunity to perform and make a good living.

Be Thankful for What You Got

America has always tried to enforce a rule of gratitude in regard to its Black citizens, forcing them to be grateful even though history would suggest that there was very little for which to be really grateful. If anything, they should have been hostile. But hostility often leaves one incarcerated or dead. And so some individuals, like the jazz musicians and the basketball players, often expressed their hostility through their music or their play. Then there were the constant demands of the predominantly White fans, who created an unfortunate power balance between themselves and those who were performing. Since slavery there has always been something potentially subordinate about performing for White audiences that continues to underlie this relationship.

To "perform for the White man" has never been easy, but by the '70s it was certainly becoming profitable. One needed to make a living, and playing basketball was even better than simply making a living because you received large sums of money and much visibility to boot. At a certain point the individuals in question figure out that they are the reason that the stands are packed, and they begin to understand that their talent is what draws people to the game. They begin to recognize their value to their team, to the ownership, to the fans, and to the public at large. This realization along with the money gives them leverage. Yet they are not always celebrated and embraced; they are instead expected to perform, expected to tap dance, and to do so with "the quickness," as they say.

This all breeds a great deal of resentment among the performers, too, I would say. White audiences tend to exhibit love/hate tendencies in this arrangement: they love your performance, but they hate you, as demonstrated by the continued racism prevalent in society. The same people who cheer you at the arena can be the same ones who deny you access in the real world. At some level the performers in question know that if they could not blow a horn or dunk a basketball, they would be just another nigger in the eyes of many. They have to process all of this and still play basketball. There is a need to separate oneself so as to avoid the confusion and in order to maintain some sense of one's own identity, to stand apart and aloof from the maddening crush of the expectant audience. Consequently, their outward performance often obscures their inner confusion.

Whatever one's feelings may be about drug usage, the proliferation of cocaine in the NBA in the late '70s/early '80s highlights a complex situation. The league was on one hand becoming increasingly Black, not only in terms of population but in style of play and in its overall aesthetic. This newly visible Black presence was somewhat offset though by the looming cloud of racially based perceptions that informed the population shift. As far as the public was concerned, these players were criminals and not indulgent artists. They were not afforded that much liberty. Some of the individuals in question, Bernard King for one, had even been implicated in some criminal activities. Thus the NBA came to be thought of as simply another example of Black criminality, not unlike those Black criminals represented in other aspects of society across the news media.

There was an increasingly perceived link between Blackness and crime that began to circulate, especially after all of the urban unrest that engulfed many city centers during the late '60s and early '70s. America never recognized this as a response to the harsh conditions of urban life or as the rebuttal to years of racial discrimination, but instead the nation simply chose to focus on the criminal aspect of such incidents, reinforcing the racist underpinning of such misconceived thoughts. Of course, not all Black people were criminals, nor were all NBA players dope fiends. But such is the basis of racism in this country. The acts of a few often come to represent the entire race, whereas the deeds of one White person are thought to represent only that individual.

Don't Let It Go to Your Head

A cursory look back on the NBA of the late '70s/early '80s reveals that the cocaine culture was everywhere that the stars and the elite gathered, not just in NBA locker rooms. Cocaine at the time was not considered to be physically addictive. It was widely used by many in Hollywood and the music industry. Mainstream magazines like *People*, *Time*, and *Newsweek* all featured stories about the pervasive impact of cocaine in the entertainment industry during this time. That palace of hedonism, Studio 54, has become an American landmark because of its unique mix of celebrity, dope, and disco. Popular movies and television programs like Brian De Palma's *Scarface* and Michael Mann's *Miami Vice* chronicled the maddening reach of cocaine's influence and its related criminal subculture.

There were also zeitgeist books like Jay McInerny's *Bright Lights, Big City* and Bret Easton Ellis' *Less than Zero*, which played out elaborate cocaine-fueled fantasies of excess set in places like Manhattan and Beverly Hills. Even respected, thought-to-be-legitimate businessmen like former General Motors executive John DeLorean, who had gone off to start his own short-lived car company, DeLorean Motors, was caught in a cocaine sting operation.

The emerging culture of hip hop, itself rooted in the expression of the urban poor, would deliver a scathing critique of coke indulgence in the song "White Lines" by Grandmaster Flash and the Furious Five. Hip hop's influence was not yet fully articulated through basketball at this time, as the sport was still, as I have described it, motivated by a jazz aesthetic. Nonetheless, "White Lines" demonstrated that this coke culture had crossed a number of boundaries, as hip hop was resolutely a genre of music emerging from and speaking to the masses of inner-city youth, whose ghetto life background was not unlike the background of several of the NBA's more prominent stars. In time the music's youthful appeal would become an integral part of this specific urban basketball experience.

The point is, cocaine was represented to be literally everywhere that there were stars, wannabe stars, their sycophants, and money. No longer the province of the elite though, this cocaine culture was increasingly taking hold throughout America, across the board, as "White Lines" indicates. The NBA simply served as one of the sites where that culture had surfaced. Contrary to perceptions at the time, it was not the only site nor was it the most excessive of these sites; it was simply one among many.

KIND OF BLUE

In a sports culture where people had become accustomed to embracing and celebrating the two-fisted White American male who drank too much alcohol but was celebrated for his hard living and where Black players tended to be seen and not heard, the new NBA was something different. It offered a new kind of hero, a Black urban hero, whose increased visibility in this increasingly individual sport was such that it caused America to shudder. What to do with young Black men who have money?

This situation had never actually occurred before. The jazz musicians were visible only to those who were really interested in jazz, and that number was never as large as the culture's influence. Plus, jazz musicians might have made a good living, but with the exception of Miles Davis and a few noted others, jazz musicians never really made a lot of money.

So the new NBA was the test case, the start-up, the first place where there was really a collection of Black bodies and an increasing amount of money to pay them. Like any first generation, they suffered more than future generations, both in perception and in overall plight. Yet they did lay the groundwork for what was to come, future generations of Black 'ballers who would challenge the status quo just by their very presence. Spencer Haywood, David Thompson, and the others were representative of what could happen when someone mixed the potent combination of fame, wealth, and an addictive personality, using racism and poverty as the accelerant. Their narratives would eventually come to comprise a long list of Black athletes who seemed to have it made and then fucked it all up. Their tragic tales of high and low would become the standard motif in the proliferation of such things. Many are called to play the game, to make the money, to live the life, but few are chosen to survive it all.

These tragic stories would, in some way, suggest that the life for a Black man was never easy, even when it appeared to be so. The allure of NBA fame and wealth was again like the red cape of a bullfight, held out and waved so as to seduce the Black bull into charging headfirst in the direction of the White establishment. This seduction, however, could only lead to destruction once one got past the momentary deceptiveness of the cape. Though some Black bulls would fare better than others, the bottom line is that the objective of the bullfight is to kill the bull, no matter how inspired or entertaining it might appear in the performance.

For these reasons this first generation to inherit what had become a Black league were like martyrs for the cause. They sacrificed themselves so that one day in the future their NBA descendants, now freshly liberated by hip hop, could reap the benefits that were born out of their initial struggle to rep a Black league still confined to the demands of a White imagination. Unfortunately, there were casualties in the process. These melodramatic lives revealed an American nightmare disguised as the dream. They were not living out the "American Dream"; instead they attempted to create an imaginary dreamscape for themselves through drug use, only to be shaken awake to a more troubling reality.

However, as is often the case, their personal struggles as well as their triumphs helped push the game in a forward direction. Haywood, Thompson, and many others are representative of a generation who laid the groundwork for the present generation of hip hop–inspired 'ballers. This is evident in the reverence that is constantly displayed now between our present generation and their basketball forefathers. Nike, for one, has capitalized on the idea of the "old school" in numerous television commercials that make direct links between the players of the '70s and those who now play the game. Many of today's players have learned from the past while still being reverent of it. As future generations of NBA 'ballers emerged, it became apparent that the pursuit of this ephemeral notion of the "American Dream" was in the process of being transformed, though it would take some time before we would be able to see the fruits of this early labor.

That Ol' Black Magic and the Great White Hope
Basketball and Race in the Reagan Era

Mourning in America

The year 1980 will forever live as a year of significant change in American culture. Most noteworthy that year was, of course, the election of former B actor Ronald Reagan to the office of the president. Reagan would establish himself and his ideas as both iconic and definitive of the era, often referred to as the Reagan '80s or, better yet, the Reagan era. The election of Reagan signaled the beginning of a new America, a much more conservative and reactionary one, one that now seemed fully recovered from America's brief flirtation with liberalism in the 1960s and '70s.

Reagan was anything but left. While his policies have been celebrated as helping to end the Cold War, for many African Americans and other minorities, Reaganism was far from being something to celebrate. For many disenfranchised people it was about weeping and a gnashing of teeth. His embrace of an ultraconservative social agenda in turn made it acceptable, even popular, to be openly hostile toward race issues, and this cast a dark cloud, no pun intended, over the prospects for any real Black advancement into the vortex of American society.

Though Reagan declared his election the dawning of a new day, "Morning in America," for most Black people it was more like "Mourning in America." Many in America may want to remember Reagan in the Sir Galahad tradition, as the gallant knight riding in on the white horse to save the day. His arrival for those whom Curtis Mayfield once called "we people who are darker than blue" was similar to a knight riding in all right. This knight was not so gallant, however; no, this knight was something akin to those knights who rode in at the conclusion of D. W. Griffiths' landmark racist film *Birth of a Nation*.

———

IN ADDITION TO REAGAN, another shift was taking place in 1980 that would forever redefine the game of basketball, introducing a new era and a new brand of racial politics to the equation as well. As the number of Black players in the game rose dramatically in the '70s, the NBA's old habits were slowly giving way to something more modern. The game was in transition, a moment when it was becoming a Black game, not only in terms of population but in terms of style as well as perception.

While Reagan made it increasingly difficult to speak out on the continued injustices fostered by racism in America, basketball became a very visible stage where the racial politics of the time were being continually played out in the open. At the center of the battle were two competitors and two cities that perfectly fit the bill.

The presence of Earvin "Magic" Johnson of the Los Angeles Lakers and Larry Bird of the Boston Celtics would mark another in a long line of sports episodes involving the mythical battle over racial superiority. In this regard, the notion of a "great White hope" is of the utmost significance in understanding the image of Larry Bird and the way that fans and the media reacted to him. Going all the way back to the days of the explosive Black heavyweight champion Jack Johnson, this idea of a great White hope would consume the American imagination. As it played out in the NBA with Magic and Bird, it offered us a prolonged series of events that would forever change the way we think about basketball.

Ultimately, this competition between the two went well beyond the basketball court. Indeed, my interest in the two transcends the actual games themselves. The on-court battles were simply the tip of the iceberg. It is the entire era and all of its racial images that makes this contrast so interesting. Magic, Bird, Reagan, Los Angeles, Boston, and the overall representation of race in popular culture from the '80s was very much like a well-written script that included all of the proper elements for an edge-of-your-seat thriller. In the end, Magic and Bird were simply vessels who helped bring society's confrontational attitudes about race out into the open, while making them somewhat more palatable because the issues were being presented through basketball.

Lethal Weapon

When the 1980 NBA finals started, everyone knew that the two preeminent superstars of the game were Dr. J of the Philadelphia 76ers and the Los Angeles Lakers' dominant center, Kareem Abdul-Jabbar. By the time the finals ended, a third name had been added to the top of that list. The name was Earvin "Magic" Johnson. He was a twenty-year-old rookie who was no longer the man-sitting-next-to-the-man. He, at least for the time being, occupied that space all by himself.

Kareem was the Lakers' dominant player primarily by virtue of his legendary "sky hook" shot. Having stepped on the national scene as Lew Alcindor back at UCLA, now, some ten years later, the Sunni Muslim convert had changed his name and, over time, changed the game. His youthful athleticism had led the Milwaukee Bucks to a title in the early '70s, and the Lakers had given up the farm to acquire him in the late '70s in one of the most talked about trades in NBA history. However, it was not until the Lakers signed Magic, after only two years at Michigan State, that they were able to reach the finals and compete for a title. For all of Kareem's greatness, he needed someone to get him the ball, and Magic was the guy for the job.

The sky hook was arguably the most difficult shot to defend in basketball. Because Kareem was so tall, at seven-foot-two, he already posed a challenge for any defender. But the sky hook made it even worse. Considering the long reach of Kareem's arms combined with a slight jump off the floor and the arc of the ball at its height, a defender often found himself trying to contest a shot that was almost impossible to block.

That shot was as automatic as clockwork and it dropped nearly every time Kareem put it up, especially near the end of the game. It was about as unstoppable as one could imagine. Pat Riley, Kareem's coach for much of the '80s, once said that although Michael Jordan was the game's most dominant player, he did not possess the game's most lethal weapon. That distinction, he said, was reserved for Kareem's sky hook.

Kareem was living up to his billing in the 1980 finals. Averaging thirty-plus points a game and giving the Lakers a slight edge with a three-games-to-two lead in the series, Kareem had seemed to be the difference, and his continued dominant play would be essential if the Lakers were going to prevail. Yet during game five in Los Angeles, Kareem injured his ankle and would most certainly miss the next game in Philadelphia.

Conventional basketball wisdom assumed that the Lakers did not have a chance against the 76ers without Kareem, certainly not in Philadelphia. Having no chance of winning in Philly, everyone thought that the Lakers would in essence forfeit game five and rest Kareem so he could be back on the court for the decisive game seven in LA. Kareem did not even make the trip to Philly. As it turned out, he did not need to.

The Prince of Darkness

It was announced at some point before game six started that Magic, a rookie, would take Kareem's place and "jump center" as they called it. That meant he would stand at midcourt and vie for the opening tip against Philly's center. Magic was only six-foot-nine, small for a center but a giant in relation to his regular position, point guard. The idea of Magic jumping center was even more evidence to many that the Lakers did not have a snowball's chance in hell of winning this game. Many saw this as a gimmick and regarded it as a move of desperation on the part of the Lakers. What is also ironic about this in hindsight is that later on in his career Magic would often be ridiculed for his chronic inability to jump into the stratosphere like many of the younger, more athletic players coming up in the Michael Jordan era.

Not only did Magic win the opening tip, but he, in effect, won the game. Playing in place of the injured Kareem, Magic, the rookie, went on to dominate nearly every aspect of the game as the Lakers rolled to an easy victory behind Magic's amazing coming-out party: 42 points, 15 rebounds, and 7 assists. It was as though no one else was on the court. Even though another former UCLA standout, Jamal Wilkes, put up 37 points with that funny-looking over-the-head shot, Magic was the decisive factor. At some point in that game he had played virtually every position on the floor. As a matter of fact, what he did was obliterate the need for the traditional five positions. He turned it into a playground game, where the most dominant players defy position and instead work to dominate the entire court.

Basketball had been somewhat formal in its approach before this, though the inclusion of a new breed of player from the ABA had loosened things up a bit. Guards were smaller outside players while forwards and centers worked inside. Each position had a specific function to perform, and for a team to be victorious, each member had to play his respective position. Though different from baseball or football, basketball still had its own tradition, but much of it had been developed in a previous era.

Well, on that day in 1980, Magic chunked tradition straight up in the air like the ball he hoisted in flight after the final buzzer sounded. He demonstrated that a great player was one not confined to a particular position, but one who could simply *play*, whatever the circumstances might be.

It was not lost on fans that Kareem, the venerable center, now into his second decade as a professional, had been back in Los Angeles during this monumental victory. The sky hook notwithstanding, Magic's performance had made the memory of Kareem a distant one, somewhere "outta sight, outta mind." Kareem's skills were still in good form, but this game indicated that his day would soon pass. See, Kareem, like his superstar colleague Dr. J, needed someone to get him the ball. They were helpless without a good point guard. Kareem especially needed to be set up properly, and this is what Magic had been doing for him all season long.

Kareem was dependent, but in the emerging style that Magic displayed in game six, control of the game stemmed from having the ball in your own hands, not waiting for someone else to get it to you. This old-style plodding, walking the ball up the floor and passing it to the big man in the middle, was no longer going to get the job done. No, this was too slow, too deliberate. The game now required movement, and Kareem, bless his heart, was practically immobile. He was most certainly stationary. Magic on the other hand was highly mobile, both athletically and otherwise.

Kareem was a star before the television cameras routinely covered every aspect of the game. His sullen lack of emotion was straight out of the Miles Davis school of cool. Kareem never smiled, rarely celebrated, and often had very little, if anything at all, to say. Over time he would be involved in several incidents with the public that would further these perceptions of antisocial behavior. Kareem, like Jim Brown, another of the Black athletic superstars whose era coincided with the militancy and nationalism echoed during the Black Power movement, felt that his job was to play basketball, not smile for a demanding White audience.

In the same way that Miles would often perform with his back to the audience or refuse to announce the tunes he was playing, Kareem avoided any open display of emotion whatsoever. He was not there to entertain, he was there to dominate on the basketball court, and that performance was in no way intended to appease a White fan base that had grown accustomed to Blacks catering to them and their sense of entertainment.

Kareem was no Uncle Tom. He was instead a no-nonsense Black man who refused to give the fans a little extra by smiling, preening, and outwardly celebrating. He was representative of the politically embittered Black man, that dark brooding genius of a figure that jazz had introduced to America. He was not a showman, no, he was an artist, with the sky hook as his horn, his "ax," and the basketball court as his bandstand.

Magic, though, was of a different generation. In addition to being a great basketball player, Magic was an entertainer. You heard nearly as much about Magic's magnetic smile as you did about his stunning no-look passes. Magic played the game not as though it was drudgery, not like it was even work. No, Magic played the game like it was fun, as though he was having the time of his life. Now this may seem insignificant to some, but it was far from meaningless in the overall impact that Black style and the representation of Black masculinity would have on the culture at large.

SMILING FACES, SOMETIMES
THEY DON'T TELL THE TRUTH

As evidenced by Kareem's sullen appearance, some Black men for a time had decided to retreat from the front lines in regard to the task of entertaining White audiences. At some level all of sports, as they relate to Black athletes particularly, are about a performance that goes back to the days of slavery and emerges again as a pop-cultural force with the minstrel tradition exemplified around a figure like Bert Williams. The boxer Jack Johnson worked to antagonize White people, but some would say that his preoccupation with performing for them in the end was a self-fulfilling prophecy, however contrary the acts might have otherwise been. By the time of Bill Russell, Jim Brown, Muhammad Ali, John Carlos, Tommie Smith, and then Kareem, however, the message was clear and emphatic: we are athletes, not performers, and there is a profound difference between the two.

So for Magic to take it back, as it were, to actually smile, was a stark departure from previous examples. Some attributed his smile to, and equated his rah-rah style with, the acts of a collegian. When you consider Magic's youth at the time and recognize that he could have been playing for his second NCAA title in 1980 as opposed to his first NBA title, this suggestion is not far off.

Was Magic conforming to White expectations or was he simply being himself? A smiling Black man was often thought to be what White people wanted, a veritable lawn jockey who made them feel good about themselves. This sense that surrounds the smiling Black man again dates back to slavery, but was fueled by the antics of the Black comedic actor Lincoln Perry, better known as Stepin Fetchit, in the earlier days of Hollywood. Is this what Magic was representing, especially in the immediate aftermath of Kareem's hardened persona? Or was he simply young, gifted, and Black, and enjoying every minute of it?

Dr. J had cut his famous afro when he got to Philly and the NBA. Was Magic now taking this issue of conformity to another, more stereotypical level? All these questions and many more were becoming relevant now that Magic had turned the basketball world upside down and almost single-handedly, in an LA moment, ushered in a new era in basketball and, as we would see, in American culture.

Magic Johnson would go on to become one of the most popular athletes and entertainment figures in the 1980s. His five championships with the Lakers during that time meant that he was constantly in the limelight, and his smiling persona made him an instant success with fans of all races. He eventually transcended the game itself and in doing so set the table for the cultural behemoth that Michael Jordan would become only a few years later. In this regard Magic is very closely linked to another Black icon of the '80s, Bill Cosby.

In the same way that Magic, a Black basketball player, came to demand a certain amount of crossover attention, Cosby dominated the airwaves during this same time. *The Cosby Show* was the weekly vehicle that generated his high visibility, and it was the highest rated television program during this time. Cosby himself was ubiquitous, appearing in numerous commercials, writing best-selling books, and seeming to capture the attention of the public at large by virtue of his inoffensive brand of comedy. Like the popular E. F. Hutton commercial during the time, when Cosby talked, people definitely listened.

When you consider that the 1980s was a time of intense racial disjunction, spurred by the attitude most consistently attributed to Reagan, both Magic's and Cosby's success suggests an alternative scenario. If America was thought to be so hostile to Black advancement, why were these two figures so successful with mainstream White audiences?

The point is that both figures represented the maturation of the Black celebrity figure in the era following the civil rights and Black Power movements. America by the 1980s was open to celebrating Black figures if they fit the pattern that had been designed for them. Both Magic and Cosby were associated with an acceptable, nonthreatening brand of Black entertainment, be it Magic's smile or Cosby's brand of benign comedy.

Magic was very different from the David Thompsons and Spencer Haywoods before him, and he was even quite distinct from his own teammate, Kareem. These individuals had been informed by equal parts Black Power and jazz, and they were also the first generation to be fully able to claim a dominance in the league. This was an uneasy position, and many of them have the scars to prove it. Having come up between the political and the popular, they had to negotiate these treacherous waters without the aid of a guide. They were on their own, with no real predecessors to inform their journey.

These earlier figures were removed from the fray, distant and thought to be aloof; they were really uncomfortable being around White people and unsure of what to say and do. The public was also in a moment of transition, not knowing what to do with these newly minted Black superstars whose money and status made them something quite different to ponder than had been the case previously.

Showtime

Magic and his generation could benefit from the failures of the previous generation. America seemed ready to accept Black celebrities if they conformed to the prevailing standards prescribed for them. Magic was a thrill to watch, and he made it easy for people to like him off the court as well. Playing in LA, Magic was the star of stars in the city of stars. Unlike a movie star who might have a big movie released once, at most twice a year, Magic was onstage constantly during the NBA season, and because the Lakers were so good during this time, the season lasted for months on end.

Indeed, as a Laker, Magic appeared nightly in one of the longest-running productions of the '80s. His face would come to be as familiar as any of the more prominent Hollywood stars who might attend a Lakers game. He gave meaning to the Lakers brand of basketball, which was of course known as "Showtime." Perfectly fitting both Magic's style and the style of the city in which he played, "Showtime" was not simply basketball anymore, it was entertainment, and entertainment at the highest level. And for this reason it required the consummate showman, and this was without a doubt Mr. Magic himself.

Yet it would be incorrect to assert that Magic was popular simply because he smiled for a fawning White audience. Magic was a great basketball player and an even better stylist of the game. What made him so spectacular was his ability to do things with the basketball that few others were able to do. He was a leader, a floor general, and he ran the fast break better than anyone else who played the game. Magic excelled at creating situations for his teammates, making them better players simply by virtue of being on the court with him. His basketball IQ, as it were, reached the level of genius, and here he in his play openly refuted any possible suggestion that Black athletes were physical but not intellectual.

In addition to all of this, he was amazing to watch. His style was part Harlem Globetrotter, part smooth soul singer. His creative abilities and improvisational skills set him apart from all others. Though he was far from the best shooter, defender, or rebounder, his hustle, desire, and determination meant that he would find a way to beat you, however unorthodox his method might be.

The classic example of this was his "baby sky hook," which he used to beat the Boston Celtics in an important game during the 1987 series. By this time Kareem had started to fade as a dominant force, and Magic, never really known as a great shooter, was increasingly being asked to shoulder more of the scoring burden. On a last-second in-bounds pass, Magic took the lane and, though barely getting off the ground, put up a miniature version of Kareem's famous hook and won this important game in the Boston Garden, setting the stage for a decisive home court victory and a fifth championship a few days later.

Magic also mastered several aspects of the game at once, and in so doing forced the league and the public to begin keeping track of a new statistic known as the "triple double," getting double figures in three different areas of the game. Now basketball purists will tell you that the great Cincinnati and Milwaukee player Oscar Robertson averaged triple doubles during his career in the 1960s, and this is true. Yet by the 1980s, Magic made this statistic a regular part of his performance, and in doing so made others pay attention to this as a mark of distinction. For Magic a triple double was often achieved with points, rebounds, and assists. Because of his six-foot-nine frame he was able to dominate almost every aspect of the game, offense and defense, full court or half court. It seemed like he was all over the place, all at once, like he was playing five positions simultaneously, and controlling the tempo in each one.

He was not as athletically gifted as Dr. J, whose balletlike moves to the hole were legendary. He was not the pure shooter that Larry Bird was either, able to take a jump shot from anywhere on the court with a high probability of making it; though he would become a very good shooter near the abrupt end to his career. What he was as a basketball player was smart. Magic took advantage of what he had, and his unending desire and enthusiasm for the game made him an immovable object and unstoppable force.

His passes were the work of a true magician, as evidenced by his famous "no look" pass, working a now-you-see-it-now-you-don't sleight of hand that left opposing players guessing, looking confused and befuddled. In addition, he was unselfish, looking to make a teammate better before ever thinking about himself. Magic was the ultimate team player, and this in spite of the fact that Black players were often stereotyped as being selfish and concerned only with individual accomplishments.

Moreover, Magic did it with a style and flair that was perfectly suited for the entertainment-minded Hollywood crowd. He put on a show every night. Magic made the game something to watch for both the basketball purist and the nonfan alike. He transcended the game and made it something akin to a good movie or a popular song. Basketball was now entertainment and suitable for a mass audience, so different from what it had been only a few years before.

Whereas the generations before Magic were like bebop and post-bop jazz musicians playing music mainly for the hip and knowledgeable, and ultimately for other musicians, Magic was like that generation of R&B or soul singers who took the music to the masses, without compromising any substance in the process.

Pop Star

In this regard, Magic would become synonymous with another emerging pop icon of that time, Michael Jackson. In the early 1980s, Jackson was moving away from his R&B base and veering off into the land of pop. Though he had come to prominence as a young performer with his brothers in the very popular Jackson Five, he ventured out on his own in the late '70s, and by the early '80s was on his way to becoming the most popular entertainer in the world. Jackson's classic Quincy Jones–produced album *Off the Wall* (1979) set the stage for that mega-cultural moment known as *Thriller* in 1982. Though Jackson was Black, his immense talents had propelled him to superstar status, crossing every racial boundary one could possibly construct.

Over time, Jackson's physical features would change from Black to something unknown, and his weird personal life would come to dominate any media attention accorded him. Nonetheless, he was the king of pop, not jazz, not R&B, not even rock. Pop implied that he offered a little something for everyone. He was ubiquitous, and representative of the heights that a Black performer could reach, and at some point, he also became representative of the depths to which they could descend.

Magic had reached the same peak, and in 1991 would fall to the same depths when he announced that he had contracted the HIV virus. His sexual popularity had become a curse, in the same way that his racial transcendence had at one time been a blessing. Here, Magic had become a stereotype of the highest order. He was the overly sexed Black lothario/jock whose avaricious appetite for sex had made him a poster boy for the possible pitfalls of being young, Black, rich and famous. Whereas drugs or taxes had been the downfall of many a Black athlete before him, sex consumed Magic and forced an abrupt end to his reign as NBA superstar and cultural icon. One was forced to ask, is it possible to be Black and successful without some unforeseen monster lurking in the depths waiting for the right time to pounce on your world?

Nonetheless, Magic was a phenomenon, especially in the 1980s, when he demonstrated that Black performers could achieve mainstream visibility at levels previously considered unattainable. The Magic example proved that a Black man could be a crossover star. He could make money, have fame, and play the game that he loved with flair and distinction.

Magic has also been able to maintain that star status even in his retirement from the game. He is now a highly regarded entrepreneur who has successfully linked his name to such profitable ventures as the Magic Johnson movie theater chain and Starbucks coffee. There is even talk that Magic might run for mayor of Los Angeles at some future time, having already demonstrated his political clout in helping elect LA's current mayor, James Hahn, in 2001.

The point here is that Magic was a product of his time, a crossover Black star who was quite easily embraced by fans of all races and maybe more important, a Black crossover star who came along at a time when you could actually cash in on this fame and widespread societal acceptance. Far from being a threat, Magic has proven himself endearing to many. This popularity has remained in spite of his association with the HIV virus, which has negatively stigmatized so many others.

Before Magic came along it was not clear if this type of popularity was possible, certainly not in basketball anyway. Sure, O. J. Simpson had done it on the gridiron, but that was football, America's most popular spectator sport. Magic had done it in a game that was relatively new to the American sports psyche, and he had done it in a league that only a few years before had been derided as a collection of overpaid Black drug addicts. He pushed the game from the margins to the center, and he did so with a flourish that was uniquely his.

Yet, Magic could not have done all of this on his own. His rise to popularity, and the concurrent rise of basketball in the public mind, was closely connected to the battles between Magic and his Boston Celtic nemesis Larry Bird, whose working-class White disposition assisted in giving the public a racial Cold War. Their on-court battles allowed the culture at large to play out one of its age-old struggles over racial superiority through the vehicle of basketball.

THE RETURN OF THE GREAT WHITE HOPE

When Jack Johnson became heavyweight champion of the world in 1908, a massive panic struck those who were interested in maintaining the mythical sovereignty of the White race. Johnson, the larger-than-life Black champion who was a great fighter and seemingly unbeatable, was far from being deferent or docile, the mode of behavior considered most appropriate for a Black man of his time. Instead he was loud, boisterous, and wanted everyone to know that he had defied convention and become the champion in spite of the overt racism of the day. Johnson once reportedly said, "I'm Black, and they'll never let me forget it. I'm Black alright, and I'll never let them forget it."

Over time Johnson would become the patron saint of the "rebellious" Black athlete. His superior abilities allowed him the luxury of almost certain victory. His personality meant that he was not shy about showing the world this superiority over his White opponents. Outside the ring, Johnson routinely flouted a convention of the time that could have had him killed on the spot. He openly showcased his numerous relationships, sexual and otherwise, with White women. Johnson was a provocateur of the highest order. He was a defiant Black man whose unparalleled athletic abilities were matched only by his equally strident penchant for rejecting the constraints normally imposed on Black citizens of that time. He was, as the parlance went in that day, "a nigger who needed to be bought down a notch or two." He was, according to the racist dictates of that moment, a Black man who needed to be "put in his place."

Therefore, the White power brokers and those who saw the opportunity to make a quick buck off of what was thought to be a momentary racial aberration sought to end Johnson's gloating while getting paid in the process. To this end they drafted "Gentleman" Jim Jeffries, a retired White champion, to carry the mantle of his race and defeat this Black menace known as Jack Johnson. Gentleman Jim came to be known as

"The Great White Hope." Actually he was considered the only hope that Whites had in stopping Johnson and restoring the sovereignty of the assumed superior race.

Though time would bring about a change and people would begin to use more subtle language in describing their intentions, sports in America continued to be one of the places where these surrogate race wars would be played out over time. As successful Black athletes used sports to expose the racial inequities present throughout other aspects of American life, even in boxing there remained a challenge to what had at once been a White domain, especially considering that the racism of the time often would not even allow integrated competition.

By the 1980s it was clear to all who cared to pay attention that Whites were not only losing the battle, but they were also, with frequent visibility, losing the war. Black athletes were consistently excellent in whatever pursuits they tried to conquer, and this dominance was spreading rapidly. But White athletes and White society had yet to throw in the towel. Larry Bird was waiting in the wings.

If Ronald Reagan did anything, it was create a culture where White men could, without challenge for the most part, stand forth on their Whiteness in an unabashed state of clear and present racial superiority. Not that this posture had ever dissipated. But the 1960s and '70s had at least brought a vocal critique to bear on unquestioned White male dominance. Between the cries of the Black nationalists and the feminists, White men were said to be under assault, though the metaphoric White Man had not relinquished any real power during this time. After years of unquestioned dominance, and then a few moments of rhetorical critique, it might have seemed to some that things had shifted, but in actuality they had not. White men remained dominant in American society, it's just that their dominance was now being questioned, however subtly. In reality their power remained unchallenged, though. Perception, however, is another thing.

By the 1980s, as I have established previously, the game of basketball was thought to be a game played by urban Black men. Many had argued that the game was being destroyed by greedy, dope-addicted Black prima donnas who were not acting in the spirit of the true American sportsman. The game was nowhere on the cultural radar screen. It did not have the tradition of baseball or the popularity of football. It was an urban game, devoid of any connection to the previous ways in which people watched and vicariously participated in sports.

What better way then to attract interest and propel this sport into its nadir than an old-fashioned surrogate race war? Black man versus White, urban versus rural, East versus West, nigger versus poor White trash. The stage was set, and the respective combatants, the Jack Johnson and Jim Jeffries of their day, were now Magic Johnson and Larry Bird.

The Magic/Bird rivalry, which started during the 1979 NCAA finals when Johnson's Michigan State team soundly defeated Bird's Indiana State crew, was about to command a great deal of interest throughout the 1980s. Yet the impetus for the race war–like composition of this battle had really been underscored in a fictional space set in the late 1970s.

In 1976, the fabled bicentennial, the overwhelmingly popular film *Rocky* had created a scenario where an arrogant, over-the-top, wealthy Black champion was pitted against a poor, working-class ethnic stiff named Rocky Balboa. Rocky had little chance of winning, but his heart, desire, and refusal to give up pushed champion Apollo Creed to the limit. Eventually, in a subsequent film, Rocky would overtake Apollo.

Here it was: an overmatched White fighter, who had far fewer "natural" athletic gifts and even fewer advantages, had pulled himself up by his proverbial bootstraps and put his best foot forward so as to conquer the reigning Black hero, Creed, who struck quite a close resemblance to Muhammad Ali. This was a time when Ali was still largely hated by many Whites, well before his public image would undergo a complete rehabilitation and he would become one of America's greatest living heroes, made politically palatable for a modern age. The '70s were a time when Ali remained an ungrateful militant Black charlatan in the minds of many.

The fictional character of Apollo Creed then was far from heroic. He was hated and the film worked to clown him, using garish Americana as a stylish overture to suggest Creed's overall disregard for proper decorum. Creed was represented as making fun of America during this historic time, and it was Rocky, the "true" American, who in the fictional-ized world of cinema came to represent the aspirations of all the White people who had been forced to the sidelines when the forward move-ment of civil rights and Black Power made their way into the cultural psyche. Rocky's success would come to stand for the fictional triumph of White goodness over the real-life success of the Black athletes who were by this time routinely dominating the sports pages.

What is really interesting here is that Rocky did not even win the fight in the first film. Yet he did win by standing his ground in a fight he was for all intents and purposes supposed to lose resoundingly. His tri-umph was what sportscasters often call a "moral victory," one where de-sire overcomes skill, where heart means more than ability, where "wanting it more" cancels out any perceived athletic advantage. Add to all this a little luck, and the White man now had a chance against this supreme physical specimen, the Black man. Notice how in all of this, traits most associated with the definition of what made a good American were celebrated when attached to the White competitor.

Rocky was the White man who, like his Italian-immigrant forefa-thers, had come to America and survived through a two-fisted combi-nation of hard work and an abiding sense of "smarts" mustered under the constant demands of America's industrial ethos. Stunningly, some-how in all of this the hardworking efforts of Black slaves had been trans-formed into lazy, trifling, passivity of ungrateful and undeserving niggers who simply wanted, in the infamous words of onetime secretary of agri-culture Earl Butts, "a new pair of shoes, a tight pussy, and a warm place to shit."

———

IN THE EARLY 1980s boxing produced a real-life Rocky and veritable "Great White Hope" in the form of Gerry Cooney, a giant of a man with few fights who had managed to climb to the top of the heavyweight ranks and got a chance to go against reigning heavyweight champion Larry Holmes. This fight coincided with the release of *Rocky 3*, a film in which the now undisputed champion Rocky, having defeated Apollo Creed in the previous film, must fend off the brutal Clubber Lange, played by Mr. T. The film continued to play on the underlying racism of the "Great White Fictional Hope." After convincingly disposing with Lange, Rocky would move on to defeat the Communist menace Ivan Drago during the last days of the Reagan Cold War in *Rocky 4*.

In the real-life version, Cooney hit Holmes several times below the belt in the fight, but Holmes finally knocked him out. Had the fight gone to a decision, Cooney could very likely have been the first White American heavyweight champion since Rocky Marciano in the 1950s. Cooney virtually disappeared after the Holmes fight.

To this day, one can visit the First Union Center in Philadelphia and find a statue of the fictional character Rocky that is larger than the statue of the real-life Dr. J. *Rocky* looms large in the fiction of America, and its influence has often been used to usurp the real-life accomplishments of prominent Black athletes. This is a subtle though poignant example of the way that popular myths and fiction can come to inform the overall public psyche on an issue. In this case, the continued desire to see White dominance in sports has been supplemented by a fictional narrative, a Hollywood film, which can ultimately have more power than some true-to-life events.

In a direct connection to basketball and Larry Bird, the 1986 film *Hoosiers* plays straight into this sense of White cultural mythmaking. Bird, of course, hails from French Lick, Indiana, and was often referred to as the "hick from French Lick" in his NBA playing days. Bird even dedicated his championship victory over the Lakers in 1984 to his college town of Terre Haute.

Bird had originally gone to the state's premier basketball institution, Indiana University, in Bloomington, to play for coach Bobby Knight. The coach, troubled in his later years, had in the '70s represented the vanguard of college coaching, especially after the retirement of John Wooden at UCLA. Knight had assembled a stellar group of players in the mid-'70s and had gone on to win the NCAA national championship in 1976 by going undefeated through the whole season. He is the last college coach to have accomplished this amazing feat.

Knight was soon regarded as a genius by the media and his coaching peers, though over time his bellicose ways would go out of style and he would, by the end of his tenure at Indiana in 2000, be something akin to a laughingstock for his refusal to adjust his clearly out-of-control abusive personality to modern times. Yet in the mid-'70s he was highly respected and certainly the coach any Indiana high school player would die to play for.

Well, as the story goes, Bird and Knight did not click. Bird departed Indiana not long after enrolling there and ended up back home in French Lick working on a garbage truck. He eventually enrolled at Indiana State, a smaller school in Terre Haute. From there he would go on to fame, leading the obscure Sycamores to the NCAA finals against Magic and the Michigan State Spartans in 1979.

Bird epitomized the rural Indiana player highlighted in *Hoosiers*. The climax of the film showcases the all-White rural protagonists, coached by Gene Hackman, as they go against a team from South Bend whose players are all Black. Hackman's Hoosiers win the game in dramatic fashion, showing that teamwork, adherence to fundamentals, and a hardened work ethic can overcome the many physical disadvantages that this smaller all-White team faces when going against their menacing Black opponents.

Though the film was set in the 1950s and is supposedly based on a true story, its recasting as a film text in the 1980s is not a coincidence. Released at a time when the game of basketball was being increasingly dominated by Black players who generally played a very urban style in which athleticism was key, *Hoosiers* undercuts this by suggesting that this all-White team from a previous era, though overmatched physically, could overcome adversity through their mental superiority. In addition, this idea of hard work, and maybe more important, teamwork, was also instrumental in dethroning the individualistic nature of streetball that had come to be discussed often by White sportscasters in regard to Black athletes.

White basketball players, with Bird as the most often used example, tended to be discussed as not having the physical ability to compete with the Black players, who were in turn thought to be "natural" athletes. Black athletes, according to this logic, were "born" to be great athletes. This idea of being "natural," of course, is closely linked to a notion of the primitive, and this is informed by centuries of biological racism which purports that Black people are of a different physical strain and potentially subhuman. This thinking also suggests that Black players do not have to work at being good athletes, they simply are that way coming out of their mother's womb, bouncing a basketball in this case. Their success is expected, and whenever they do not accomplish their goals, they are immediately castigated because their natural abilities are thought to be such an overwhelming advantage.

There were some key sports incidents in the late 1980s that articulated this sentiment. First, old-time Los Angeles Dodger executive Al Campanis during an infamous interview on *Nightline* told Ted Koppel that Blacks did not the have the "necessities," as he put it, to be good coaches. In other words, their mental capacity was such that they did not possess the intelligence to be managers of baseball teams. Campanis went on to articulate a long list of stereotypes about Black athletes and eventually caused a firestorm of controversy with his words.

Not long afterward, CBS sportscaster Jimmy "The Greek" Snyder, a onetime bookie, spoke in an interview about how Black players were taking over sports, leaving little for White people to do. He went on to describe the way that Black athletes had been "bred" for success in sports during slavery. This, too, touched off a controversial war of words in the press and public.

Both of these comments revealed long-held assumptions about Black athletes in the White imagination. Unable to explain or accept the way that Black athletes were indeed "taking over" many sports, White media pundits and sportscasters began laying out the "natural athlete" thesis so as to compensate for the racial changes taking place in the sporting world. Black athletes had seized the moment, and with sports being one of the few arenas where Black people were allowed to excel based on their merits, it made sense that large numbers would choose that line of work. Yet this situation exposed the lingering racist tenets present in American society, so it became necessary for White society to undermine this increasing dominance by forwarding these myths of racial and cultural superiority.

The acceptance of this "natural athlete" thesis, which, I must add, was cosigned by many Black people as well, seemed to be a compliment, but it is instead an insult when you really break down all the implications. If this were true, how do you account for the millions of Black people who have never played a sport? Why then are not all Black people who pursue sports successful? This biological argument is without any merit, though it is an argument that keeps getting recycled. Culture is the key to understanding this phenomenon, but few want to accept it as such.

Larry Bird would go on to immense success as a member of the Boston Celtics. Throughout his tenure, his team would win three championships while Bird garnered many individual awards and unparalleled attention. The composition of his team, the Boston Celtics, was predominantly White also. It had amassed a great deal of attention over the years and was by this time, without a doubt, the team with the most storied NBA history and tradition. Though much of this had been accomplished when the NBA was still in its infancy, the Celtics did feature one of the game's first real Black superstars in the great Bill Russell, who at a certain point in later years also served as the team's head coach. By the late 1970s, though, the Celtics were a bad team and, like the rest of the league, not paid much attention to.

The Celtics decided to draft Larry Bird after his junior year at Indiana State. Though he still had another year of college eligibility, the Celtics took him off the market. Not long after, the NBA changed the rules and made this sort of early draft transaction illegal. Well, by the time Bird arrived in Boston, he was their savior. Having played in that legendary NCAA final game against Michigan State, Bird had been preordained a superstar already. His rural White background was a perfect fit in Boston, where the working-class Whiteness of that city had long served as the dominant cultural influence.

Boston's racial strife had also been well documented, going back to the bloody school busing battles of the 1970s. This was a town considered very hostile to African Americans, and their lily-White team and fans did nothing to contradict this assumption. Yes, there were Black players on the Celtics—even a Black head coach in KC Jones—but they were generally seen and not heard. This was especially true after the

Celtics drafted Bird's partner in crime a few years later, the lanky, Frankenstein-like Kevin McHale. As a matter of fact, one of the team's best Black players, Robert Parrish, was called "The Chief," as in "cigar store Indian chief," due to his consistent stoicism. He was about as silent and invisible as one could be.

Boston's three championships in the 1980s included only one against their West Coast rivals, the Lakers. Boston defeated the Lakers in the '84 series. This victory continued a streak of championship wins that the Celtic teams of old held over the Lakers. It was supposedly indicative of that so-called "Celtic Mystic." For many, the Celtics' triumph over a much more talented Laker team was proof that their substance was superior to the Lakers' style; the attendant racial implications here are obvious.

This is especially true when considering that several crucial mistakes by Magic Johnson throughout the series, near the end of certain games, made it seem that Bird and his team were clearly better able to rise to the occasion than their flashy "Showtime" counterparts. The Lakers, however, were victorious the following season and again against the Celtics in '87. Both of these series ended in six games.

The Celtics defeated the Houston Rockets for their two other championships. While the Celtics battled with Philadelphia for the Eastern Conference crown in the early 1980s, and the Detroit Pistons in the late 1980s, they were always thought of as the team to beat in the East. The Lakers assumed similar status in the West. Yet on two occasions, in 1981 and 1986, the vaunted Lakers were underachievers and lost to the Rockets in the conference finals, giving Boston a cakewalk to the NBA championship. In other words, Boston, which made the finals a total of five times in the 1980s, beat the Lakers only once in head-to-head competition, and that series took seven games to settle. The Lakers on the other hand won five championships throughout the 1980s and were in the finals a total of seven times throughout the decade.

While Boston was certainly a very good team during this time, they were not nearly as dominant a team as the Lakers, yet history seems to have woven the two teams together in memory. In my mind, two of those championships against Houston should have an asterisk by them, as Houston was clearly several steps below the Lakers and Boston in terms of being a dominant team. In 1981, Magic Johnson spent a great deal of time injured and shot an infamous airball in a losing effort against Houston in the first round of the playoffs. In 1986 the Lakers were swept by the "twin towers," Ralph Sampson and Hakeem Olajuwan, in a playoff upset. Boston went on to defeat Houston on both occasions.

Ebony and Ivory

This is not to make an excuse for the Lakers. It is however an attempt to properly contextualize the Magic/Bird rivalry and the issues of race as illuminated by popular culture from that time period. Magic was clearly the more successful of the two, though history will forever link the two players as equals. This is somewhat demeaning, as Magic should be accorded his proper place without having to share the throne. That notwithstanding, Magic and Bird's significance to the game and the culture at large is tied to the way that their presence on the scene could be read as symbolic of the racial and cultural difficulties still circulating through America, especially in the conservative heyday of the Reagan '80s. America loves a race war, especially when it is hidden under the shroud of a basketball game.

Bird fought a valiant fight for the working-class White male ideal that was losing ground in sports but remained all-powerful in society at large. The great White hope aspect of his image was helped along by both fictional and nonfictional images that worked to maintain a White ideal. Bird was being referred to as "Larry Legend" long before his playing days were over. It was as though, like Rocky, by simply being able to compete with the perceived natural superiority of the Black athlete he had won already.

Magic proved to be a worthy opponent and in the end he was not so much of a societal threat that his success needed to be contained. He was an acceptable, entertaining Black man, in the image of Cosby and the self-proclaimed "King of Pop," Michael Jackson, who went on to a very high level of cultural acclaim as well, much more so than the somewhat reclusive Bird.

Magic's connection to Bird helped bring basketball into the mainstream of American life as the issues tied to both of them were irresistible to the public at large. Basketball had come of age, and in this maturity it was obvious that race would always be a part of the game's representation, regardless of how much anyone might have wanted to suppress it or act like it had nothing to do with the game's appeal.

The racial connotations involved in the Magic/Bird rivalry would by 2003 seem to be ancient history. Though the two players often went at it on the court, it was Bird who introduced Magic when he was inducted into the Basketball Hall of Fame in 2002, indicating for the record that the two would be forever linked. Their rivalry and the racial issues that informed it in the 1980s were now routinely discussed as indicative of a bygone era. Many even laughed at the absurdity of it all.

While much of the racial discourse of their time was embedded in the competition of these two great players, the issues of both race and class would burst out in the open by the time hip hop came to have an influence on the way the game was played, around the late '80s. Now the racial discussion often has to do with style, and when you consider that there are so few White American players of prominence in the game at this present time, this sort of overt Black/White racial conflict has all but disappeared. What has emerged in its place is public consternation over the hip hop generation and how its members refuse to conform.

Though Magic at one point had his coach, Paul Westhead, fired, his success, and the success of his future coach Pat Riley, seemed to obfuscate this act of power. Allen Iverson, on the other hand, has gotten as much grief for openly disagreeing with his coach Larry Brown as he has praise for his play on the court. What for Magic was a move that got lost in the sands of the historical hourglass, for Iverson is an albatross of perceived insubordination that he and members of his hip hop generation must bear at all times.

As the NBA became more and more of a Black league, class and style were the hot-button issues as race seemed to be subsumed or at least made into the norm with this new majority. The Magic/Bird era was a nice transition on the way to hip hop becoming such a significant factor in influencing the game. Though hip hop would seem to have little to do with the Magic/Bird era, the racial conflict that engulfed this time certainly set the table for what was to come sometime later.

Chocolate City
Georgetown and the
Intelligent Hoodlums

THe PLaYeRS' BaLL

The 1982 NCAA championship game between North Carolina and Georgetown will live in history as the beginning of a new era in college basketball. Though the Michigan State/Indiana State game from 1979, only a few years earlier, had introduced the world to Magic and Bird, this 1982 contest would feature several prominent individuals who would expand the game even further.

Most people will remember this game as the one where a freshman out of Wilmington, North Carolina, Michael Jordan, hit what turned out to be the game-winning shot. Jordan was the third option on a great Carolina team that featured James Worthy and Sam Perkins, among others. Yet coach Dean Smith decided that the youngster should take the last shot. Jordan stepped up and made it, launching what would become the greatest career in the history of basketball to date.

Though Jordan was the superstar-in-waiting that night, he was not the only superstar-to-be on the court. Worthy, of course, would go on to become known as "Big Game" James during his stellar career with the Lakers, and Perkins would have a long NBA tenure himself. On the other side of the ball, though, Georgetown center Patrick Ewing and his coach

John Thompson, one of the few Black men coaching a major college program, would achieve their share of fame as well.

Actually the emergence of the Georgetown basketball program, spurred by the dominance of Ewing and the visibility of Thompson, was an equally important story that came to the public's attention that night. Between 1982 and 1985, Georgetown would play in three NCAA championship finals, winning in 1984. Following this, they would also be a perennial powerhouse for many years to come.

TOO BLACK, TOO STRONG

What was important that night in 1982 was the way that Georgetown went about establishing its identity as a basketball team. Georgetown had never been known as a college basketball power. Thompson took over a squad in the early '70s that had won only three games the previous year. Yet by the early '80s his Georgetown team had reached the Final Four, and they were on their way to a long, successful run as the "beast of the East."

Ewing, a seven-foot freshman out of Boston's Ridge and Latin high school, by way of Jamaica, was the main reason the Hoyas were playing in the finals. Ewing was an imposing center who fit right in with Thompson's rugged style of play. Thompson had been a backup center to Celtic great Bill Russell for a few years in Boston back in the 1960s, and there he learned the art of playing defense from one of the true masters. Thompson built his team around defense, and Ewing, known for his shot-blocking ability, was the centerpiece. Georgetown's stifling defense sent opponents shuddering as they were often unable to get a shot off, and if and when they did, Ewing was waiting in the wings to block what desperate shot they were able to attempt.

In that North Carolina game that night in '82, Ewing went after nearly every shot they put up and got called for goaltending five times. Nearly every time a Carolina player came down the lane, Ewing would reject his shot. The shots he did not reject, he certainly altered. Though he was called for goaltending each time, which meant that Carolina was still awarded the baskets, Ewing's point had been made: abandon hope, all who enter here! Fuggedaboutit! There would be no trespassing in that lane, not on that night.

Ewing sent a message, as they say. As Thompson said after the game, he had no problem with the goaltending, though each call awarded points to the opponent, because he wanted Ewing to create "a consciousness," so that Carolina would think twice before coming down the lane. Ewing, through his actions, told the Carolina team that if they wanted to win the basketball game, they had better find another way to do so because the lane was closed for business.

The point here is that Ewing's intimidating style of play set a tone for the game and for the rest of his career at Georgetown. This idea of creating a consciousness clearly spelled out that Thompson as a coach and Ewing as a player were not only interested in winning, but winning through the use of mental as well as physical dominance. Ewing assumed a posture that was hard and defiant, possibly an indication of what was to come when the hip hop aesthetic would take over some years later. Consider then that Ewing and his team were like that classic Ice Cube distinction, "the wrong niggas to fuck with."

Ewing, unlike, say, Magic Johnson, never smiled. He possessed a trademark scowl that made his work on the court seem that much more threatening. Ewing's strong African-like facial features were such that he looked mad all the time, even if he was not. His demeanor was as hard as his game.

This is important because Magic Johnson, as I have said earlier, always smiled, and the smile became a part of his engaging appeal. Isiah Thomas, who had won an NCAA championship with Indiana in 1981, also smiled a great deal. They were both affable figures who seemed to do their job with a great deal of joy while certainly being very passionate about it. Ewing, though, was not of this ilk. He seemed to find nothing funny. It was not a laughing matter. Ewing's presence on the basketball court resembled what the great hip hop laureate Rakim would say, "I ain't no joke." Indeed.

All of this is relevant because, as I alluded to earlier with Magic

Johnson, the smiling had always been expected of Black men who appeared to perform for White audiences. Louis Armstrong got to be an American icon because he did it, while Miles Davis got to be infamous some years later because he refused to do it. It was as though the smile made you more palatable and less threatening for a White audience that wanted to be entertained but not scared.

Well, by the early 1980s, young Black men had become the face of menace in America. Often projected as murderous criminals on the nightly news, in popular films, and in society as a whole, Black men were without a doubt public enemy number one. This became increasingly true as the Reagan era took hold. So, for this reason, many Black men who were interested in making it in the hostile world of America would smile so as to lessen the perceived threat and to make smooth their path as much as possible. Not Ewing, and not his coach John Thompson, either.

Ewing represented a change. He went about doing his work as though he got no joy out of it at all. It was business, and he went about it in a businesslike manner. He shunned all excess, all pretense, and went out to destroy his opponents with the grace of an ax murderer. There was something very blue-collar about the way that Ewing controlled the defensive end of the basketball court. Yet even there, he managed to do so with a bit of style.

Normally, blocked shots are potentially unadorned. A player puts up a shot, it gets rejected, and the game goes on. Sometimes there is a dramatic block at a crucial point in the game, and that is exciting, but for the most part blocks are not that compelling a part of the game. Ewing though, like Bill Russell before him, added another dimension to the block. It was as though Ewing caught the shot, held it for a quick split second, and then threw it back, something like the way an outfielder throws a baseball. Not only did Ewing block your shot, he rejected it so much so that there would often be a collective sigh from the audience when this happened. It was as though he was telling his opponents to "get the fuck outta here" wherever he rejected their paltry offering. There was something quite demonstrative going on here, and this formed the basis of Georgetown's identity; this and John Thompson.

Fear of a Black Planet

Georgetown is a well-regarded private Jesuit university located in the nation's capital, Washington, DC, counting among its notable graduates former president Bill Clinton. Georgetown is not a Black school like another DC institution, Howard University, yet you would not know this by looking at the composition of the Georgetown basketball team. The Hoyas were predominantly an all-Black squad, but they were not the first.

The all-Black, Don Haskins–coached Texas Western team had won the NCAA championship in 1966 against legendary coach Adolph Rupp and his consciously all-White Kentucky team. From that moment forward, college basketball became an integrated affair for the most part. Eventually, Black players would come to dominate most rosters as time passed. Adolph Rupp, nicknamed The Baron, had once taken his team off the floor because his opponents featured Black players, and this went against his Southern code of conduct. Texas Western, which would later be called the University of Texas at El Paso (UTEP), not only beat Kentucky that night, but also made a statement to the world about the limits of segregation and the ridiculous posture that Rupp had assumed.

By the early '80s many of the best teams were predominantly Black, but Georgetown took it to another level. The fact that Georgetown's squad was all Black may seem insignificant by today's standards, now that the face of basketball is overwhelmingly Black and Blackness is the norm, but in the early 1980s there were still a large number of White players who were highly visible in the game. Though Black players were dominant at this time, there were always a few prominent White players demanding their share of attention, too.

Chris Mullin, for instance, was a prominent member of the St. John's team and a vigilant foe during Georgetown's reign as "beast of the East" in the early to mid-'80s. The Villanova team that upset Georgetown in the 1985 finals featured several key White players on its squad as well. Duke, a team that would emerge in the mid-'80s as one of the game's more dominant programs, always featured a team filled with White players in their frequent trips to the Final Four. In other words, there would certainly be a nice collection of White players on virtually every major college team bench, and generally a few starters to boot, and possibly a White star, depending on the team.

Georgetown though was different. Throughout the '80s the Hoyas would generally feature a team that was all Black, from the first starter to the last man on the bench. This was bolstered, of course, by the looming presence of Thompson, the coach, one of the few Black men to head a successful, big-time college basketball program.

Not only was John Thompson a Black man, he was a giant. Thompson stood something like six-foot-ten and weighed three-hundred-plus pounds. He was a commanding presence no doubt, bigger than many of his players. Thompson often joked that one of the reasons he was able to land prized recruit Ewing was that he was the only coach in the country who could look him straight in the eye. So here was this giant of a Black man who, like his star pupil Ewing, refused to smile, standing on the sidelines with a long white towel draped over his shoulder, which was there, some would have said, to wipe up the blood. Like all great college coaches, Thompson was as much a part of the team as any of those guys playing on the court. He was the man, in no uncertain terms.

So here they were, the Georgetown Hoyas. Their fans talked about something known as "Hoya Paranoia," which most effectively captured what playing against them was like, a paranoid schizophrenic fit. When the Hoyas clamped down on a team, as they did in the second half of the Final Four game in 1984 against Kentucky, for instance, it was all over.

Now all of this "paranoia" was undoubtedly also connected to the overwhelming Blackness of the team itself. These were Black men playing in the place that George Clinton once called "Chocolate City" due to its large Black population, and doing things in a manner that would come to rub many in the mainstream basketball media establishment the wrong way. They were strong young Black men in an urban environment whose defiant no-nonsense attitude and approach to the game did not go over too well with a media used to seeing much more deferent Black male images and teams that featured more White players.

Over time, Georgetown would come to assume the unofficial title of "Black America's Team" due to the predominance of Black players and their articulation of Blackness on the basketball court. Thompson began recruiting players like Ed Sprigg, who had been a DC postman, and Michael Graham, who was in my opinion one of the first "thug life" players to emerge on the national scene. Graham, with his menacing defense, aggressive, high-energy, physical style, intimidating scowl, roughhouse play, and shaved head—even before Michael Jordan—was an integral part of the system, especially for the 1984 championship team. Then, suddenly, Graham was declared academically ineligible by Thompson, and he seemed to disappear into the night, never to be seen again in a Georgetown uniform. Though Graham was an important member of the Georgetown team, Thompson did not hesitate to drop him when he did not live up to academic expectations. Many college programs would have found an unlawful way to maintain a player of Graham's caliber. Thompson however was unwavering in his attempts to maintain high academic standards for his players, and he had no problem dismissing one of his best players for failing to live up to these standards.

Nike also began designing a popular gray and blue basketball shoe made especially for Georgetown that went over quite well with youth throughout the inner city. In addition, the Starter Company, makers of ubiquitous baseball-style jackets, had a big hit on their hands when they began selling the Georgetown Hoya insignia. In other words, the Georgetown team became known as a "Black" team, both on and off the court.

Georgetown's unique urban style was also articulated by Ewing himself. The Georgetown center always wore a T-shirt under his Georgetown tank top. Ewing began wearing the T-shirt underneath his jersey as a way of heading off the colds he often caught due to excess perspiration. This practical use of the T-shirt soon became a style statement copied by many other college players, like Graham, and also by young players on the playgrounds of America as well.

Georgetown's home games became so popular that the team often played in Washington's Capital Center, home of the NBA Washington Bullets, as the crowds became too big to fit into the tiny gym on the university's campus. The Hoyas were not only a good college basketball team, they were a major attraction. They began to infuse the often-staid game of college basketball with a certain energy, an energy rooted in their distinct display of Black style. The Hoyas were of the same school as the Blaxploitation heroes of the 1970s. To paraphrase the famous line from *Shaft*, "they say these cats the Hoyas are some bad muthas . . . shut yo mouth."

Their reputation preceded them. They were "hard" when they came on the scene. They made their mark by representing the Black man as no one to "fuck with." They epitomized an urban style of basketball in a college setting where this had not been a successful endeavor before. The Hoyas, led by Thompson, were something America had to this point not seen in an athletic endeavor: a group of strong, aggressive, unapologetic Black men who would just as well knock your ass down as speak to you. For many the Hoyas were America's worst nightmare, packaged as a college basketball team.

This critical mass of Black men also foreshadowed the arrival of hip hop and its relationship to the game of basketball. Hip hop has often intimidated many because, at its core, it is a site defined by large gatherings of Black men. Georgetown demonstrated this on a basketball court, and in doing so exposed many of the latent fears and perceptions still harbored in this society against Black men, particularly when they gather in numbers. Georgetown, like hip hop, never attempted to minimize these fears by softening its image. The Hoyas used these negative perceptions against them as a form of intimidation. The team could be called an early version of "niggas with attitude," and this image certainly fueled much of the animosity against them.

Georgetown was certainly popular with African Americans though. In that way they were like the baseball Dodgers, a team that drew the support of many Black people for a long time because it was the first team to integrate the game when they hired Jackie Robinson. Yet the

Hoyas were not nearly as popular with the mainstream media, who often saw them as a bunch of renegade "ringers" who were there only to play basketball and who otherwise had no business being in college.

Increasingly, the discourse around the Hoyas had to do with affirming the negative stereotypes of Black male hostility so widely circulated in the media. This imagery was eventually coupled with a conversation gaining increased momentum in college circles, which had to do with the academic integrity and preparedness of Black kids from the ghetto for the scholastic rigors of college life. Often it was suggested that the types of athletes Georgetown recruited were not qualified to attend such a university, and the NCAA, the governing arm of college sports, began implementing a series of rule changes that were supposed to emphasize the "student" in the phrase "student athlete."

Get Your Mind Right

From the early 1980s through the 1990s the NCAA began implementing a series of "propositions," numbered at various times 16, 42, and 48. Each new proposition was somehow connected to the others in either "improving" or replacing the previous proposition's intentions. These measures would restrict the enrollment of athletes in universities based primarily on the scores they achieved on a standardized test, but also to some extent on grade point average. This overemphasis on standardized test scores though was where the real racial component of the propositions had their effect. This would have an especially profound impact on Black players from impoverished backgrounds.

The SAT and ACT are the standardized tests that universities use in making their admission decisions. For years many have argued that the tests are culturally biased. Their focus favors those students who have enjoyed the best possible high school education while making it quite difficult for those not fortunate enough to have attended private schools or strong public schools. To use a standardized test assumes that there is a common standard across America in the quality of education that one might receive. This of course is not the case. Those individuals who tend to excel at sports, especially Black athletes, tend to come from lower-class, inner-city neighborhoods where there is clearly an overall lack of quality in education.

Though there are of course exceptions to the rule, many of these individuals are not prepared to take these tests, which require highly skilled preparation in order to do well on them. To use this as the standard is then creating a disadvantage for those not able to attend the best, most highly funded schools. In addition, it furthers the racist perception that while Black athletes may be physically superior "natural athletes," at the same time they are thought of as mentally inferior individuals. This, of course, was always juxtaposed against White players, who were said to have little athletic ability but possessed the desire and capacity for hard work to overcome these limitations.

The impact of these propositions is best understood when connected to Georgetown. Thompson always stressed that his players were students first and athletes second. To emphasize this, he even had the team's chief academic adviser sit on the bench during games. His program had a very high graduation rate also. Thompson argued that he was trying to give young, urban Black men an opportunity to receive a college education who would have never had that opportunity otherwise.

At one point in the late 1980s, John Thompson staged a walkout before one of his team's games to protest what he saw as the unfair application of these propositions. It was as though the NCAA wanted to send a message. The gatekeepers were saying there were too many Black players dominating the game now, and though they could not control what went on in the pros, they were determined to restore some diversity to the college game. Diversity here seemed to mean adding more White players to the mix. Well, over time, the propositions would take their toll, and one would see fewer and fewer inner-city Black athletes given the opportunity to start college with their class, and some would never get the chance at all. These propositions are what eventually made the college game less attractive for many would-be 'ballers, and this made the leap straight from high school to the pros increasingly common by the mid-'90s.

THE FALL

By the mid-1990s, Georgetown had started to fade. Though they remained a good basketball team, they were not nearly as dominant or as feared as they had been in the 1980s. Thompson's influence began to wane; the Hoyas no longer induced paranoia. The undoing of Thompson began back in the late 1980s when he was selected to coach the US Olympic basketball team in the 1988 Olympic Games in Seoul, Korea. Though many suggested that Thompson's success at Georgetown merited his selection as Olympic coach, others were not so sure.

A well-known sportscaster in the 1980s wondered aloud whether Thompson would select any White players for the team, leveling the perverted charge of "reverse racism" that Thompson often heard because of his penchant for all-Black teams. In addition, many questioned Thompson's strategy as a coach. Thompson sort of broke ranks on this issue, too. He decided that he was not going to assemble an "all-star" team of the best college players, as he put it, which was the way Olympic teams were typically composed.

Instead, Thompson insisted on building a "team" by gathering a group of role players who fit Thompson's own style, a group made similar to the teams he regularly put on the floor at Georgetown. It seemed as though Thompson was trying to prove to his critics that he was able to win by doing things his own way. But this public ego battle did little to achieve the goal of assembling a team that could compete for a gold medal at the games. This was especially the case considering that by this time many of the Eastern European squads were increasingly catching up to the once exclusively dominant Americans.

With players like Jeff Greyer and Bimbo Coles on the Olympic squad, the US did not stand a chance against the stronger teams from the Soviet Union and other countries that had developed a knack for playing the American game. The US did not win the gold medal in basketball for the first time since 1972. This 1988 squad is the only team that can truly be said to have lost the gold medal on the court, as opposed to the 1972 team, which lost a controversial game when the timekeeper reset the game clock three times until the Soviets finally emerged victorious.

Thompson's team was terrible, his players badly mismatched against the professionals who played for some of the foreign squads. It was Thompson's headstrong tactics that resulted in humiliation at the 1988 games. This loss was such an embarrassment for the US that it prompted the use of American professional basketball players for all subsequent Olympic teams, including the inaugural incarnation of the Dream Team in 1992.

THE RACE MAN AND THUG LIFE

By the mid-1990s, Thompson was running out of tricks. He had one final bright moment when he landed a troubled young man out of Hampton, Virginia, named Allen Iverson. Thompson had gained his reputation as a defensive coach who specialized in training big men. There was Ewing, of course, but later on Thompson would coach Alonzo Mourning and Dikembe Mutombo, two centers who played in that same defense-first mode that Bill Russell had established with the Celtics long before. Thompson appropriated Russell's style and, just like the great method-acting coach Lee Strasberg, who appropriated Stanislavsky, Thompson taught his star pupils the method of Russell.

Yet Iverson was a small guard, not a big man like the others. In addition, Iverson represented a new generation of Black basketball player, one who had come of age in the Reagan '80s and who had been nurtured under the hard-edged dictates of hip hop culture. Iverson had been involved in a racially charged brawl with several of his friends and a group of White youngsters at a bowling alley while in high school, and this resulted in his imprisonment. Though it appeared that the charges against Iverson and company were racially motivated, the star athlete sat wasting away in a prison cell. He was eventually pardoned by Virginia governor Douglas Wilder and his conviction was overturned, but the damage was done.

Iverson was hardened for life, and his less-than-sacrosanct image was about to contrast sharply with the image of the players Thompson had historically featured on his team. Though the two had what appeared to be a good relationship while together at Georgetown, Iverson bolted after two years and went to the NBA. Normally Thompson's players stayed for their full four years. But Iverson represented a new day.

Though Thompson had regularly recruited players from troubled backgrounds while coaching at Georgetown, he found in Iverson a new breed, one who, like his peers from the hip hop generation, did things as they wished without the requisite fear of authority that Thompson had engendered in an older generation of players. Iverson had a great career at Georgetown, but it was clear that his desire to do his own thing in the NBA was more important than learning more lessons from Thompson.

Again, while recognizing that Iverson and Thompson had a good relationship, it was clear that Thompson ultimately had little to offer a player from a generation he knew very little about. Iverson leaving Georgetown after two years signaled, to some, the demise of John Thompson's influence as a college coach. The game was passing him by. He had had his moment back in the 1980s, but times were changing and that old-school race man attitude that had once worked was no longer viable with a new hip hop generation that found little reason to celebrate the past exploits of those thought to be worthy of honor. When Allen Iverson decided to leave Georgetown for the NBA, it was the end of an era. Thompson, who in the 1980s had seemed a revolutionary of sorts with his penchant for featuring teams reeking of uncompromising Blackness, was now, by the 1990s, an old-school disciplinarian teaching from an old-school lesson plan.

Blackness in Transition

What is important about Georgetown is the fact that John Thompson along with players like Patrick Ewing represented the changing face of college basketball. Thompson recruited the kind of inner-city players who would a few years earlier have been playing for White coaches.

There were coaches like Al Maguire at Marquette and Ray Meyer at DePaul who specialized in recruiting inner-city players to compete for their Catholic school teams. This in and of itself did not seem so threatening. Yet when all these Black inner-city players were playing for Thompson, a Black coach, it gave off an entirely different image. Georgetown was Black in color, but also Black in style. The Hoyas added a dimension of aggressive physical play to the game that made them seem even that much more of a threat to the White social order of college basketball.

When considering that there has always been this lingering suspicion about urban Black men and their perceived propensity for violence, Thompson instructed his team to play in a way that reinforced this perception. He did not shy away from the stereotype; he embraced it. This style was such that while it intimidated a lot of people, it also endeared the Hoyas to a large number of Black fans who otherwise would probably not have paid much attention to the game. This is evidenced by the way that Georgetown's athletic gear became the hottest apparel on inner-city streets. The game that the Hoyas played was very much like the game played on playground blacktops all over urban America. Thompson simply put it front and center, and made it a mainstream attraction.

The visibility of the Georgetown Hoyas also put streetball, in this organized NCAA context, on the map. College basketball had always been able to maintain a certain sense of its scholastic perception because it was always a coach's game, as opposed to a player's game like the one being played in the NBA. With John Thompson, a successful Black coach at Georgetown's helm, this was still a coach's game, but now the coach was Black and able to offer a different style. The prominence of the Hoyas during such a difficult time relative to racial politics put Blackness right around the corner from the Reagan White House. Though they may have won only one championship, Georgetown during this time won the war of style so rooted in an urban sense of Black identity. This perception not only changed college ball, it also proved, for all those who did not believe, that the game was on its way to becoming a Black thing entirely. It was too early to honestly call

Georgetown a hip hop team, but they certainly established a style that was the antecedent to what would become a basketball connection to hip hop culture in the future. Though this transition to hip hop was still a few years away, Georgetown did a great deal to point the indicator in that direction.

I Am
Hip Hop, the Individual, and the Culture of Michael Jordan

I ball for real / y'all niggaz is Sam Bowie /
and with the third pick / I made the earth sick /
M.J., hem Jay / fade away perfect.
— JAY-Z, "Hola Hovito"

AN AUDIENCE WITH THE KING

What is there to say about Michael Jordan that has not already been said? There is no question that Jordan is one of the most ubiquitous American icons ever, or that his presence and visibility have for quite some time far transcended the game of basketball. Jordan used basketball to become one of the most talked-about figures in the history of American popular culture. Indeed, what else is there to say that some sportswriter, pundit, academic, or person on the street has not said so many times before?

Well, this is not intended as another praise song for Michael Jordan, nor is it a diss. Yet if one is serious about discussing the NBA's ascent into the stratosphere of popular culture, it seems that a great deal of that conversation must include a discussion of Jordan's overwhelming influence in getting people to watch basketball who otherwise would have never been interested. At a certain point in the 1990s, when Jordan began to regularly win championships and every award imaginable, when his face was everywhere you could possibly imagine, to me, he became boring. We clearly knew that no one could compete with him, that not a soul was more successful or for that matter more culturally relevant. He was the undisputed king and we all knew it, because we all helped put him there. So, what was the point? The man was his own world, and it seemed that we were just borrowing time while occupying space in that world.

I have never been a bandwagoneer. If I am honest, I, for a long time, found Jordan to be just a bit too popular, too easily accepted by a mainstream White society that only grudgingly accepted the kind of Black people that they saw fit. Jordan and I are of the same generation. We were in college at the same time. I feel some connection to him by virtue of this, not to mention my own personal experience with him back in the late '80s. I was working at the NBC affiliate WDIV-TV in Detroit covering basketball. At the time the Detroit Pistons were playing at the Pontiac Silverdome, about a thirty-five-mile distance from the downtown studios. I was charged with covering the game, doing the postgame interviews, and then transmitting these interviews back downtown via satellite so that they could be used for the sports section of the evening news telecast.

One particular Easter Sunday, I got the assignment to cover the Pistons and Bulls. This was a time before the whole world knew Jordan. Real basketball heads knew him from back in the day at North Carolina, and he was certainly beginning to turn many heads with his amazing play in the NBA, but he was not yet the worldwide media icon he would become in the '90s. Well, on this Easter Sunday, Jordan dropped sixty-three points on the Pistons. It was truly amazing, mind-boggling even. I had witnessed an astounding performance. And I knew I had witnessed history, like having been in the audience when Paul Robeson sang or when Miles Davis had blown his horn. Jordan had done something incredible, and I was fortunate to be there to see it with my own eyes.

Before this game, one of the White guys back at the station had instructed me to ask Jordan for one of his shoes, so that they could show it on air. This of course was never going to happen. I would never humiliate myself in this manner. This guy had no idea how dehumanizing it was to ask another man for one of his shoes, especially another Black man. This was something a White guy could do if he wanted to, but there was no way I was going to ask Jordan for one of his shoes. That would have violated the often unspoken though well-known code between Black men, "Never ride another man's jock." That was the quickest way to lose respect.

In the elaborate game that we often play between race and masculinity, it was fine for some starstruck White boy to ask a Black athlete for something like that, as they were secretly thought to be sycophants anyway. In a way this was some sort of weird payback for Black men so often having been on the powerless end of the racial equation. It was thought that White adulation was one of the few ways that one could feel empowered. The thinking went something like this: "You have denied us everything else in society, so you will pay a heavy price for your love of our music or our excellence in sports." In the words of the late great Biggie Smalls, "They just fans like De Niro, Wesley."

Now when the situation was "brotha to brotha," as this one was, none of this "dick ridin'" as it is often referred to was allowed. To fully emphasize these codes of Black masculinity, one need only listen to the rapper Ice Cube tell a drooling fan on one of his albums to "get off my dick nigga, and tell yo bitch to come here." While none of this might inspire a feminist embrace, it is at the root of most communication between Black men, particularly those who would inhabit the space that I did on that Easter Sunday afternoon.

I was not going to ask Jordan for anything other than an interview, which was what I was there for in the first place. In order for me to be taken seriously, Jordan needed to see me as his equal—another brotha tryin' to do his thing—not as some starstruck fan seeking autographs or other such paraphernalia. So as I made my way to the Bulls locker room after the game, I kept all of this in perspective, trying to mentally prepare for the task of interviewing him that lay ahead.

At some point I had read that Jordan had said when asked who he thought did the best job of guarding him that the Pistons' Joe Dumars was his most rigorous defender. Now as I'm on my way to the interview, I know that Jordan has answered so many of the same questions so many times that he would probably be tired of the redundancy by the time I got there to ask mine. My first responsibility was to cover the local team, and I had to get Pistons coach Chuck Daly's reaction before I could go over to the Bulls locker room. This was not an ordinary story though, as it is not every day that you see someone score sixty-three points. So Jordan's actions did merit a reshuffling of priorities.

When I arrived in the Bulls locker room, the deafening sound of J. J. Fad's "Supersonic" was engulfing the entire space. Charles Oakley, Jordan's valet in those days, and Horace Grant were deeply into the music, as no one wanted to speak with them or anyone else on the team for that matter on this particular day. Jordan was the man, without a doubt. He was the front, back, and center of attention. As I approached the mob scene that still engulfed Jordan, I needed to find a way to stand out, so as to get something good rather than just sticking the microphone in the crowd and recording what everyone else was asking. The crowd was in front of him, so I went to the side. When there was a brief break in the action, I took my shot.

"You've said in the past that Joe Dumars guarded you better than any other player in the league. But obviously, when you put up sixty-three, he couldn't have been doing too much guarding, right?" I asked. Jordan proceeded to turn away from the mob and shift squarely in my direction. He stopped talking to them and started talking to me. They all shifted their position and now they were behind me. He looked at me and responded, "Well, Joe and I have had some great battles, but the way I felt out there today, no one could stop me." We went back and forth a few more times, and then it was over, just like that. I said "Thank you" for his time, and he responded, "No, thank you!" as if to affirm the good exchange and the respect between two brothas trying to do their thing. Game recognize game, as they say.

After this, Jordan—now clearly tired of answering questions—turned toward Oakley and Grant and began bouncing to the music with them. This was a Black thing, and they had turned this locker room into their own world, complete with their own rules, so much so that the White media guys had to feel like interlopers. Jordan was not some media icon, nor was he some untouchable deity. He was a young Black man who had just done something spectacular. And he was, like the rest of the brothas in that room, myself included, just having fun and enjoying life.

This is the image of Jordan of which I am most fond. The pre-'90s Jordan, when he was a young cat in the game just trying to find his way. No unrealistic pressure, no unbelievable expectations. Just basketball and kickin' it with the fellas.

THe LIFe anD TImes OF M. JORDan

Many years later, in 1999, I had another opportunity to meet Jordan at a private session following one of his Jordan Flight School camps at the University of California, Santa Barbara. Jordan regularly holds these highly successful summer camps, which give upper-middle-class White kids controlled, close proximity to him for a week. In addition, Jordan invites several of the most promising high school players of all races from around the country to attend. That year the gathering included future NBA lottery picks Darius Miles and Dajuan Wagner, among others. There was also an assortment of celebrities in the mix including comedian Chris Tucker and several of Jordan's boys like Ron Harper and Quinn Buckner.

The camp is run by former college players who serve as the camp's counselors. These people are carefully recruited so as to provide Jordan with the best pickup game competition, which they play each night after all the little kiddies have gone to bed. So, this scene was like Jordan's private workout, and the vibe was jovial, exclusive, and yet somewhat intense, similar to what one might have expected to find at an old Ali training camp. Though I already had clearance to get into the closed-door session that night, it was still like going through Checkpoint Charlie to get past the guards.

This invitation into the private sanctum of His Airness had come in the period immediately following the release of *The Wood*, a film on which I was a producer and cowriter. I, along with the film's writer/director, Rick Famuyiwa, had been granted an audience with the king through Rick's friend, who was one of the camp counselors. In addition, my longtime friend George Raveling ran the camp for Jordan. So I was truly in the mix, as one would have to be to even get into this particular VIP room, otherwise known as the Thunderdome on the University of California at Santa Barbara campus. Having a chance to see Jordan play in this exclusive environment was like having been able to hear Miles Davis in a private practice session. This would be nothing short of amazing, or so I thought.

There was another guest in the house that night, a guest who did not seem to fit the mold of the others: Percy Miller, better known as Master P, the New Orleans rapper/ghetto mogul. P, it was rumored, had paid for several of his young relatives to attend the camp, and so he was there, as they say, on the strength of that financial gesture. Miller had already drawn a lot of attention when he pursued two ultimately unsuccessful attempts at playing professional basketball. He had tryouts with both the Toronto Raptors and the Charlotte Hornets, neither of which landed him in the league, though he made it to the final cut on both squads. P was probably not going to play pro ball, as this evening in Santa Barbara revealed. But the fact that he could add these exploits to his résumé was reason for conversation in and of itself.

Master P had made his way into the rap game by sheer force of will. Being from neither tradition-rich New York nor LA, P managed to put New Orleans on the map in the rap game by relying on some sheer P. T. Barnum–like ghetto tactics. Choosing to focus on the Southern region of the country, P had founded an empire that produced rap music, made low-budget movies, and offered 1-900 numbers. He had even started to make inroads into the field of athletic representation, attempting to establish himself as a sports agent through his No Limit company. Though No Limit would for a time represent University of Texas standout and Heisman Trophy winner Ricky Williams, who was drafted by the New Orleans Saints and signed to what was said to be one of the worst contracts ever negotiated, P, at the time, still seemed to be making moves on a major level. His name was routinely listed among some of the wealthiest entertainers of the late 1990s, and he also appeared on the *Fortune* list of the richest individuals under the age of forty.

Master P, it was rumored, had also formerly been a dope dealer.

Other rumors suggested that P was laundering money through his No Limit enterprise. While none of this speculation has ever been confirmed, the speculation has persisted. Some of this has been fueled in part by P himself, who often rapped about drug-dealing exploits in his music. On the other hand, it is important to point out that racist stereotypes often cast a suspicious eye on successful Black male entrepreneurs as to the real origins of their money. Master P has not been immune to this stereotyping. He seemed to be preoccupied with other things like building his massive empire, thus he did not seem to care about squashing such rumors.

The point is, P was a wealthy Black entrepreneur whose crass methods and thuglike persona were about as far from Jordan's pristine public image as one could ever imagine. Jordan is one of the most popular American icons ever. His image cuts across all lines of race, class, and gender. Master P on the other hand was an entertainment jack-of-all-trades whose potential limitations in any of those sectors was overshadowed by his extraordinary financial success.

In the same way that perception might suggest that a luxury goods store such as Neiman Marcus is more sophisticated than Wal-Mart, the reality of it is that Wal-Mart, however low-level and potentially lower-class it might be in terms of perception, is a financial behemoth because it has identified its customer base to be the common man and woman rather than the glittery societal elite. There are always more commoners than there are elite. Master P is like Wal-Mart then. By making his target audience the Southern ghetto dweller, he has capitalized on a market sector into which no one else has ventured. Jordan on the other hand is associated with everything mainstream, from Nike onward. Well, it was reported that P's earnings were higher than Jordan's that particular year, and there was the rub.

Jordan's camp was like a shrine, a temple of basketball, and he was the Buddha. One dare not step to the master unless he requested your presence. There was even a printed manual that instructed the camp counselors on the appropriate manner in which to approach Jordan, and when this approach was allowed. One was not to speak unless spoken to. At one point Chris Tucker, an actor associated with some of the most financially successful movies of recent years, without permission went up to ask Jordan a question. Jordan visibly ignored him as though he were just another little flunky. Everyone in attendance that night seemed to cosign Jordan as though he were an oracle; accordingly, the resentment toward Master P was quite palpable.

On the court, Jordan took every opportunity to embarrass Master P, often referring to him as "the rapper," a phrase that carried much derision. Jordan rejected P's foul calls, went out of his way to post him up, and generally made it clear that P was an unwelcome guest. We were in Michael's house.

P's behavior on the other hand was far from what one might expect from an individual associated with thug life. He was quiet, seemingly content to play basketball and not get into a mental game with Jordan. Indeed, the behavior of both men was so far from what one might expect that when I went to tell others about what I had witnessed, many of them did not believe me. They wanted to keep the image of a "good Jordan" that they already had in their heads and not have it sullied by what was clearly some unflattering behavior. Jordan in this context was acting like a prima donna, whereas he might be expected to act differently, considering that Master P was in his house, on his turf. One might also reasonably expect Jordan to have been a bit more cordial, considering that he was the one who held all the power in this situation. Instead, what I saw was that famous Jordan competitive streak that we heard so much about through the years. He would not even concede a pickup basketball game to a rapper, of all people.

The point I wish to make here is that Jordan had become something other than what he was when I first encountered him back in the late '80s. This is not meant to push some "he sold out" message, but it is to say that an individual who had once been potentially edgy had now become mainstream. No, Jordan was never edgy in the way that an Allen Iverson is edgy. They are of different generations and different mindsets. Jordon was edgy simply by bringing in a new energy to the game, a youthful energy, that went against the well-established mode of that time in the NBA.

AnoUHer Time, AnoUHer PLace

When Jordan decided to wear his Air Jordan warmup suit to the 1985 All-Star Game as a rookie instead of the standard issue All-Star warmup, he might as well have told his elders to kiss his ass. This simple style statement was perceived as Jordan being "uppity," though here the racial politics were not the same as those usually implied when this word is used. Jordan's style statement was to Isiah Thomas and Magic Johnson, two Black men who were prominent figures in the league at this time, a rejection of their authority, a dismissal of the dues they had paid. Jordan's gesture reeked of individuality and was a precursor to the dawn of an age when he as an individual would come to assume all the attention in the room at any given time.

Some years later, Jordan was the center of a mild controversy when he refused to wear a Reebok-designed warmup suit for the closing ceremonies of the 1992 Summer Olympics. As a member of the inaugural Dream Team, Jordan said that his contract with Nike prohibited him from wearing any other apparel. Though Reebok had won the clothing contract for the USA at the 1992 Olympics, Jordan suggested that his own deal with Nike superseded what many considered was his patriotic duty to wear the colors of his country.

Here, corporate culture and commercial representation trumped any national sense of identity. The individual, Jordan, was now more significant than his country. Jordan as a brand name was more viable than Jordan as a run-of-the-mill American Olympic athlete. Jordan eventually wore the Reebok suit, but was able to unzip his jacket down far enough so that the Reebok insignia was covered up.

I am suggesting here that Jordan foregrounded an image that was very much about him. This flew in the face of what many would have deemed acceptable for a modern athlete, especially in light of the "team first" mantra that still dominated sports. But Jordan was able to pull it off. He was not so much a team player in a traditional sense, like those who had been praised in the past. It was now about Team Jordan; and everyone else was told to fit into his concept.

I AM

Around the same time that Jordan was emerging as a new cultural force in basketball with his focus on the individual icon that functioned as an autobiographical emphasis of sorts, the burgeoning influence of hip hop culture was starting to gain widespread public attention. Hip hop has always been about a highly personal narrative, one that featured the individual at the center of its discourse. With its youthful energy and its focus on the self, hip hop is the perfect example with which to understand the way that basketball's torch was slowly being passed. The game was changing from the days of Magic and Bird, two great players inevitably connected to the legend of their respective team histories, to a player like Jordan, who instantly became the team himself.

Again, I am not saying that Jordan was a true hip hop 'baller in the way that Iverson and others would become later. I am saying that the early part of Jordan's pro career dovetails perfectly with hip hop being recognized in mainstream culture. For this reason, hip hop is a useful way to begin understanding Jordan's emergence on the scene. To be sure, in Jordan's later years he would become openly hostile to the influence of hip hop and the generation of hip hop 'ballers, as is often the case when an icon evolves. What I am asserting here though is that Jordan in his early years can be read against the backdrop of hip hop culture that was beginning to alter how we might read Blackness in the mid-1980s.

———

JORDAN'S MEDIA IMAGE was especially bolstered in the early days by his association with filmmaker Spike Lee. Following the success of Lee's independent feature film *She's Gotta Have It* in 1986, the emergent director would eventually go on to do several high-profile commercials for Jordan's signature Nike shoe, the Air Jordan. In these commercials, Lee's b boy from the film, character Mars Blackmon, engaged in a series of black-and-white spots with Jordan that were tailored to extol Jordan's virtues and the virtues of the new cultural status symbol, the Air Jordans. Lee's Blackmon character in the film and in these spots was firmly rooted in the culture of hip hop, and his annoying persistence—"do ya know, do ya know, do ya know?"—was such that, by contrast, Jordan's relative silence worked in his favor.

These commercials were extremely popular and helped plant Jordan's image firmly in the public imagination. Again, the connection to hip hop is not as strong as the visible connections that would emerge some years later, but it is important to remember that Jordan's early entrance into the public domain was in some ways tied to hip hop culture.

———

WHEN THE RAP GROUP Run-DMC released their single "Walk This Way" in 1986, featuring the rock band Aerosmith, who had originally recorded a version of this song, the video began appearing in high rotation on MTV. This meant that a large audience, a rock audience even, could now see the hottest musical act in hip hop, DMC. "Walk This Way" attracted an audience previously ignorant of this latest version of the Black oral tradition. DMC offered a new sense of Blackness. This was an image that b boys in NYC and hip hop fans nationwide had known for some time by that point, but was completely invisible to those who paid attention only to what was being broadcast in mainstream venues.

Central to the prominence of DMC was their unique style. They "rocked" in an all-black ensemble: black derby hats, black leather sport coats and pants, and their signature unlaced Adidas sneakers. Their high-energy performance commanded one's attention in a most arresting fashion. DMC were not passive R&B singers, or older blues or jazz musicians. They were hip hop artists who used the genre to express their own prowess and to make sure that they were never ignored. They used music to call attention to their very existence, a skill not frequently on display during the Reagan era, when Blackness was seemingly on the permanent "DL" (downlow), unless, of course, it was of the Huxtable family variety. Hip hop would become a way of being seen and, most important, of being heard when all other forces attempted to suffocate the Black voice if not deny it altogether.

In an oft-recounted famous incident, the leader of Run-DMC, Run, the younger brother of soon-to-be hip hop mogul Russell Simmons, stepped onstage at Madison Square Garden during a sold-out concert. As the urban legend goes, Run steps to the mic and yells out, "I beg yo' pardon, this is my muthafuckin' garden!" This bold statement underscores the extent to which Run-DMC and hip hop at this time were taking over territory, staking their claim to a prominent place in the culture at large.

This, to me, is what Jordan was doing in basketball as well. When one considers that many of Jordan's greatest exploits over his career were showcased in this very same Madison Square Garden, this connection has even more weight.

What makes Jordan's arrival on the NBA landscape so significant in the mid-'80s is that he brought a new style to the game itself. Jordan's game was often compared to that of Dr. J's because it was J who made the highly stylized playground game his own mark of distinction. Dr. J was known for his graceful moves to the basket and his often emphatic dunks, like the immortal cradle-rocking dunk on the Lakers in the 1982 NBA finals, or the leap from the free throw line at the 1976 ABA All-Star dunk contest. J was also a style icon, who with his original blowout afro in the '70s and the modified version of later years, his knee braces and his Converse All Stars, not only played good, but looked the part also. The Converse All Stars were so closely associated with Erving that many people simply began referring to them as "Dr. J's." So the image of Dr. J was the historical antecedent that was most often associated with Jordan in his early years.

Dr. J, of course, was the player who had made the playground acceptable in the NBA. Yet he was not the first to bring this high style to the league. Earlier players like Elgin Baylor and even Connie Hawkins in his brief career had made contributions to this particular style aesthetic. Dr. J, though, was the man who took all of this to another level and who also, upon his arrival from the more open ABA, made this improvisational manner his signature.

Jordan though was ultimately quite different from Dr. J when you really get down to it. J was quite traditional in the way he played the forward position. He was a slasher, as they now call it, and a dunker, but he needed someone like Philadelphia point guard Mo Cheeks to give him the ball in the right spot, to set him up as it were. Jordan, on the other hand, was able to handle the ball, often in a manner comparable to most point guards, and with this he could create his own shot from anywhere on the floor. He was much more of a threat than Dr. J because he did not necessarily need to be set up, he could use his ballhandling skills to set himself up. This freedom was such that it made Jordan a threat anytime he had the ball in his hands.

Early in his career Jordan was not the greatest pure shooter, but he was a great scorer because he had the ability to create a shot for himself and break down the defense from anywhere on the floor. He could bring the ball up like a point guard, he could lead and finish on the fast break, and he could stifle a defender from anywhere and go straight to the hole. What is significant about all of this is that Jordan was redefining what the positions on the floor really meant.

In a fashion similar to Magic when he played center in game six of the 1980 finals, Jordan was someone who could play three or maybe four positions with ease. Though Magic did a tremendous job jumping center against Philly, he would have been hard-pressed to play that position for a whole season because his size disadvantage would ultimately have worked against him. Jordan though was so multidimensional that he could and did play virtually every position on the floor whenever he needed to, and he was unstoppable from any of these spots. Some years later, when Jordan teamed up with Scottie Pippen, they made the positions they played interchangeable with each other.

In playground ball, positions are irrelevant. The best players simply control the flow of the game. In this context the best players often float all over the court doing whatever is necessary to win. Unlike the previously restrictive nature of NBA basketball, where people "played their position," Jordan was at the dawn of an age when people would stop even referring to the various positions by name. They began to refer to playing the "1, 2, or 3" as opposed to saying the traditional "point guard, shooting guard, or small forward." With Jordan, all of these positions were merged into a seamless whole. He could be a small forward and a shooting guard all at once. Distinct formal titles for positions were no longer necessary. Jordan made these distinctions obsolete.

This challenge to formality though was not absolute, as Jordan was inherently a strong proponent of the fundamental aspects of the game. Having learned under the college coaching guru Dean Smith at North Carolina, Jordan had a strong grasp of the game's more formal elements. Smith is even jokingly credited with being the only person who was able to "hold Jordan under 20," referring to the relatively low numbers that Jordan put up while playing within Smith's conservative system. It is this grasp of the fundamentals combined with this playground aesthetic, which I have often called the fusion of the formal and the vernacular, that has always made Jordan stand out in relation to his basketball peers.

The unique ability to embrace equal parts fundamental textbook basketball with athletic playground basketball can be argued to be similar to what the young musician Wynton Marsalis was doing in music around the same time. Marsalis was equally adept at playing both classical and jazz music, having won Grammys in both categories. Jordan and Marsalis then are of a generation of African Americans who realized that in order to be visibly successful, one needed to be versatile. Often an individual also needed to merge what at one point might have been regarded as competing interests, making those competing interests work for as opposed to against them.

Prior to this moment in basketball history it was thought that the playground style was a reflection of raw talent, but this was not equated with the honed skill that was thought to be part of what textbook ball signified. Many playground players were encouraged to rein in what was perceived as their undeveloped habits, their out-of-control physical play, and were forced to submit to the dictates of playing within an organized system. In other words, the individual was of less significance here than the overall goals of the team. The individual was subordinate and his personality potentially repressed for the sake of the system itself. No one player was thought to be above the team.

The racial implications were not lost here either. The increasingly large segment of Black players was often ordered to submit to the dictates of a White master, the coach or the organization. They were told to minimize their own individual talents for the sake of the team; similar to the way that Dooley Wilson, who played the famous Sam character in *Casablanca,* denied himself a voice while amplifying Humphrey Bogart's.

Yet Jordan, who had done this at North Carolina, was not about to do it any longer. The NBA was his coming-out party. He was going to foreground the individual and in doing so make the team that much better by sheer will and force of personality. Jordan was once quoted as saying, in response to someone spouting this old sports cliché about there being no "I" in team, that even though there was no "I" in team, there was an "I" in win, which to him was the bottom line.

Jordan's articulation of individual style here was an expression of a larger political situation inherent to the Black presence in American society. Black people were often asked, and not very gracefully either, to subordinate their own desires for the good of the country. In this equation the desires of Black people were deemed less important than the needs of society at large. The expression of Black people's desires was even thought to be counterproductive, if not downright hostile, to what society as a whole needed. In other words it was thought that Black people were not "special" and did not deserve any concessions. Black people were told to simply get in line like everyone else. This would have been fine if the playing field known as American society had been level. It, of course, was not.

So to sacrifice oneself for the sake of one's country was really a situation where you were giving away much more than you were getting in return, or as James Brown says somewhat comically in the Academy Award–winning documentary about the Ali/Foreman fight, *When We Were Kings,* this was like "paying taxes on something that you never received."

The old John Henry myth of the hardworking Black man who died trying to outwork a machine is also relevant. John Henry gave his life for nothing, except the amusement of those White people who watched him try to accomplish an impossible feat. One could also reference the real-life example of Crispus Attucks, the Black soldier who was the first soldier to die in the Revolutionary War for a country that did not even consider him a full human being.

This new generation of Black people like Jordan knew better. There was no way they were going to sacrifice themselves. If anything, Jordan was going to excel and bring everyone else along with him. He was going to assert himself, forward his identity, and do so in no uncertain terms. Jordan made it clear, it was his team. The world of the Chicago Bulls, and at a certain point the world of the NBA, would revolve around Jordan, not the other way around.

Unlike Magic or Bird, Jordan, playing for Chicago, did not have the luxury of being associated with one of the league's more storied franchises. So whatever image the Bulls were going to have, it had to be established. In times past a player like Jordan was considered selfish. And though he put up incredible numbers and made spectacular plays, a player of his type was thought to be too centered on his own statistics at the expense of the team. At that time many would frown upon a player like Jordan, and for most of Jordan's early years in the game, many skeptics doubted that he would ever be able to win a coveted championship ring like the ones that both Magic and Bird had won.

In a highly symbolic playoff game in 1986, Jordan established himself as a force to be reckoned with, beyond being regarded as simply a flamboyant dunker with his own line of shoes. Going against the venerable Boston Celtics and the much ballyhooed Celtic front line of Bird, Kevin McHale, and Robert Parrish, Jordan took the game in his hands. Jordan scored sixty-three points that day, and though the Celtics won a close game, Jordan was the one everyone was talking about afterward. He put sixty-three on the team that was thought to define this team concept. If ever there was a case of one against five, this was the day. The Bulls were terrible and yet, with Jordan shouldering the load, they almost beat the team that would go on to win the NBA championship that year.

Following this, Jordan would develop an amazing, almost uncanny penchant for winning close games at the buzzer with a series of dramatic last shots. When the Bulls met the Cleveland Cavaliers in the 1989 playoffs, it was Jordan who hit a last-second shot over Craig Ehlo and emerged leaping and repeatedly pumping his fist in a scene that has been replayed over and over again, seemingly millions of times since then. Jordan, who of course began his career at North Carolina with the game-winning shot against Georgetown, for all intents and purposes concluded his career with a scene-stealing choreographed jumper over Utah in 1998. His two comebacks from retirement notwithstanding, Jordan came in with drama and left on the same dramatic tip.

I Play For the Team I Own

With all of this, Jordan forever changed the game. He elevated the self-ish "ballhog" and transformed this character into the centerpiece of any team desiring a championship. Stellar individual talents were now thought to be a potential savior of any NBA franchise. In years to come, various superstars would often be chided for their inability to "step up" when their team needed them. Charles Oakley, for instance, once a val-ued teammate of Jordan's with the Bulls, openly criticized his new team-mate, Toronto's Vince Carter, during the 2001 playoffs for Carter's inability to take over the game—to be selfish, as it were—when the team needed it in order to be successful. No doubt Oakley saw the looming image of Jordan as the appropriate model for excellence when making his comments about Carter.

In the aftermath of Jordan, people talked about the heir to *his* throne, not the heir to the *Bulls* throne as had been the case with the Lakers and Celtics before. The league, the media, and the public went in search of the next Jordan. Who's the next Michael, they asked? Is it Grant Hill? Is it Penny Hardaway? Is it Kobe Bryant? They even called the now-forgotten Harold Miner "Baby Jordan" when he was a college star at USC. Of course, there were no heirs. The throne has thus far re-mained vacant. Team basketball had now forever been changed into building a team around a superstar, yet none of these impostors to the throne could even come close to approaching Jordan's unprecedented dominance on the court.

To me, Jordan's emergence as a basketball player is tied to the emer-gence of the individual relative to hip hop culture. In the civil rights era, Blacks had to think of themselves in group terms because the movement was geared toward "elevating the race." In the aftermath of the civil rights era, those Black people who were able to cash in were able to do so as individuals, and in so doing these individuals were able to more closely approximate the access that individuals in the mainstream took for granted.

During his career, Jordan would become a financial behemoth in his own right, furthering his individuality by possessing the means to truly be an individual in every sense of that word. This is why so many people had a difficult time trying to fit Jordan into the traditional role of the benevolent Black aspirant who "gave back" to his community, or who stood for something political relative to his popularity as a Black icon.

Jordan, unlike Muhammad Ali, for instance, came along at a time when it was *political* to be Black, wealthy, and empowered by one's own image. He was able to use this individuality not only to win basketball games but to change the terms of the culture in the process. Jordan, then, broke away from the group concept and established his own sense of being, relative not only to his Blackness, but often above and beyond his racial identity. There was now a price that one could garner from being Black and visible, thus Jordan's allegiance was to himself and not necessarily to his race.

In my mind, hip hop has always celebrated the triumph of the individual over unfortunate circumstances, and it has also foregrounded the individual in the quest to be seen and heard. Though Jordan was not hip hop per se in his politics, his timing on the NBA scene closely connects to the emergence of hip hop as the primary way of representing Blackness in the culture at large. On the other hand, Jordan's shaved head, his long shorts, and his Air Jordans all became staples of hip hop style. Just as significantly, his emergence, before there was a concerted effort to fulfill the needs of the Jordan image machine, was about bringing a youthful energy to bear on the game and the culture itself. In this regard we can see the game and the culture forever being changed by Jordan's spectacular rise to prominence.

My Detroit Playaz
Ballin' in the Motor City

Detroit / it's like Oakland / it's a
black thing / and I'm a black man.
　　　　　— TOO SHORT, "Short Dog's in the House"

THE D

Many people have forgotten about the early Michael Jordan. Many more never knew about his early incarnation as a player, set against the backdrop of hip hop as a discourse that was emerging as the most appropriate way to understand the post–civil rights era and its redefinition of Blackness. Michael Jordan in the 1980s was a very different Jordan from the one who emerged in the 1990s. It was in the '90s that Jordan became the Jordan that we now most remember; strong, determined, and invincible. Yet in those formative years, Jordan was an emerging young star trying to make a name for himself in a league still dominated by images of Magic and Bird.

It was not Magic and Bird who posed the most immediate threat to Jordan's quest for fame and championships though. No, Magic and Bird were locked in their own battles, and as the '80s progressed, the tarnish was beginning to show, however subtle, on the armor of both their squads. Jordan's most immediate nemesis happened to be due east of Chicago on Interstate 94. That, of course, was the city of Detroit, home of the Pistons.

The prominent cities on the NBA map had always been Boston and Los Angeles, with occasional references to Philadelphia and New York. Philly had the legend of Wilt Chamberlain and later Dr. J and Moses Malone. The 76ers had been to several finals in the early 1980s and were victorious in 1983, nearly sweeping all but one of their playoff series and coming close to fulfilling Moses Malone's famous "fo-fo-fo" declaration in the process. New York, on the other hand, had for years been called the "Mecca of Basketball," though the Knicks' only glory had come in the early '70s. The New York hype machine had turned that scene of Willis Reed limping out onto the court in 1970 into a moment that one could never possibly forget. This dramatic scene was repeatedly shown, but the reality of the matter was that the Knicks had not won any championships since the early '70s, and they really were not significant in terms of the league's modern history. Though they would make some noise in the 1990s, they still did not win any championships, thus further exposing that their visibility was due entirely to New York media hyperbole and the fact that the league offices were located in the city.

When talking about prominence though, especially in the mid to late '80s, Detroit was one of the last places to be mentioned in a conversation about great NBA cities. Detroit, like Jordan's Chicago, was not even on the map. This was all changing, though. In the early 1980s the Pistons had drafted Chicago native Isiah Lord Thomas III, a young star from Indiana University. Thomas was small by NBA standards, listed at six-foot-one but clearly shorter than that. He was a marvel to watch though. He brought a combination of good basketball fundamentals, having learned under the dictatorial tutelage of Bob Knight at Indiana, along with the best of the Chicago schoolyard tradition. Isiah's early NBA career was highlighted by his play in the NBA All-Star Games, where, over time, he won two MVP trophies for his spectacular playground style in that ultimate organized playground game. "Zeke," as he was often referred to around Detroit, once scored sixteen points in a ninety-second stretch during a 1984 playoff game, thereby placing himself in the company of the league's best players during this time. All this being what it was, Zeke played for a rather mediocre squad, the Pistons, who had no history or tradition on which to build. Zeke for many years was a one-man show on a ship that never got afloat enough to sink.

This would eventually change. In the mid-'80s the Pistons would begin assembling a team that eventually came to represent the epitome of the team concept while simultaneously challenging accepted notions about the image and style of the game itself. In this transition, Zeke would sacrifice his own individual statistics in the interest of making his team better.

While I still argue that Jordan marked the dawn of a new era, the Pistons were at the tail end of the previous era. Their significance lay in being able to break the Boston/LA stronghold on the NBA championship, and doing it in a way that signaled a clear departure from the way things had been done in the past.

The Pistons used an aggressive style of defense as they made their move up the ladder of the league's elite. This defense was not just aggressive, however. The Pistons used physical intimidation as their claim to fame. The team even began referring to themselves as the "Bad Boys" or on occasion "the Oakland Raiders of basketball," appropriating Raiders' insignia from the storied football franchise. This was the Pistons' away of signaling that their opponents were in for less than gracious treatment on the court. Isiah Thomas, he of Chicago's infamous West Side, often talked about learning a lot about intimidation tactics from legendary Chicago street gangs like the Black Stone Rangers, and used this knowledge in molding the Pistons into a unrivaled force.

Many of the Pistons' other players also adapted quite well to this focus on intimidation, chief among them the team's only White player of note, Bill Laimbeer. A slow White guy who certainly could not jump, Laimbeer was the epitome of a racial stereotype. Though at one point he led the league in rebounds, he was not at all physically gifted. Though he possessed a nice long-range jump shot for a man his size, he was big, slow, and clumsy. In addition he was known as a whiner, someone who chronically and dramatically complained about the referees' calls. Most important though, he was known as a "dirty" player and a cheap-shot artist, someone who would foul opposing players so hard that they often faced the potential of serious injury. It is no surprise then that Laimbeer was known around the league as the player the fans most loved to hate.

What was also interesting in the case of Laimbeer was that the media tended to make a big deal of the fact that his father was a high-ranking executive with General Motors. People often talked about the fact that Laimbeer was maybe the only player in the league who made less money than his father did. The not-so-subtle allusion here is to the assumption that most of the Black players in the league were products of single-parent ghetto households, where the father was presumed to be absent. Even in cases where the father was present, it was almost assured that he did not make more money than his NBA-salaried son did, the thinking went. So Laimbeer was defined by both race and class to be someone quite different from the majority of his fellow basketball players. Yet in the game of basketball, Laimbeer's race and class were of little benefit to him as compared to their currency in the outside world.

For all intents and purposes, Laimbeer was a thug. And he clearly enjoyed playing this role. His hard fouls and questionable tactics helped create his image as that of a White player, unlike many of his other White brethren, who could not appeal to the lingering sense of White supremacy that still informed the way that society thought about White athletes. Laimbeer's evil was then read as an extension of the team that he played on and the city that the team represented, Detroit. In the same way that Detroit was seen as the "murder capital of the world" for many years, the Pistons, and Laimbeer for sure, were seen as violent thugs who were ruining the game of basketball. Laimbeer by virtue of his style of play was effectively coded as a Black player, at least by perception. And this is also the way that the team itself was perceived, as unequivocally Black.

Don't Forget the Motor City

In the summer of 1967 the city of Detroit erupted into one of the worst race riots in American history. When overly aggressive police raided an after-hours spot, known in Detroit as a "blind pig," on Twelfth and

Clairmont Streets, the city burst into flames and added another city to the growing list of places where urban unrest was becoming a household phrase.

The city of Detroit had a long tradition of race riots, and this latest one, like those in Watts, Newark, and Chicago, underscored the changing population dynamics of urban America. Many of the nation's cities would never be seen in quite the same way again. Detroit was maybe the most extreme case of all. The city's White residents began fleeing in droves to the outlying suburbs. Soon the city would come to epitomize the notion of White flight. In a relatively short period of time Detroit became a city with an overwhelmingly Black population, contrasted with an equally overwhelming White population in the suburbs.

In 1973, Detroit elected its first Black mayor, Coleman Young, a former socialist-minded union organizer at Ford Motors who had become a state senator. Young was not only Black though. To the chagrin of his opponents he was especially outspoken and never shied away from racially charged controversy. Young, for instance, often talked about Detroit's "hostile suburbs" and clearly relished the opportunity to antagonize those Whites who were openly opposed to him and his policies. Coleman Young's tough, defiant, empowered sense of self became, for many of the Black residents of Detroit, a badge of honor, and an image with which they were completely comfortable. The mayor was one of them, and anyone who was against him was seen as either an Uncle Tom or a racist.

From his election in 1973 until he retired in 1993, Coleman Young was the face of Detroit. And his strong sense of Blackness served to distinguish the cultural politics of this city from any other. Though people have described Washington, DC, as being Chocolate City, DC is still only a district surrounded by the federal government. Blackness there is always modified by this fact. Others may celebrate the city of Atlanta as the "Black Mecca," but Atlanta is still in Georgia, and the particular history of that Southern city and state will never allow for a fully defined sense of Blackness in the way that Detroit can claim to have done.

Black people in Detroit had for a long time been working in the auto industry, and became among the first Black people to fully realize en masse something approximating the American Dream, at least in terms of material possessions. The working-class history of Black Detroit, then, provided a sizable number of people with an opportunity to buy homes and cars long before this was a possibility in some of the other cities with large Black populations. This working-class sensibility, in turn, created a sense of identity that was much more confident and, for some, much more defiant than that typically seen in Black people at the time.

A good example of this defiant sense of Black was on display as far back as 1925 when a Black Detroit doctor named Ossian Sweet returned fire on a violent, angry White mob that numbered in the thousands, and had descended on his home in an attempt to force Dr. Sweet out of their all-White neighborhood. One of the white thugs was killed and Dr. Sweet, as they say, "caught a case." Murder was the case that they gave him.

Dr. Sweet, who was reported as saying he would rather "die a man, than live a coward," was defended by the great lawyer Clarence Darrow and was eventually acquitted on grounds of self-defense. This was just one of the battles in what would be a long history of racial strife centered around housing. Yet this did not happen in the '50s or '60s, when such things were becoming routine. This was in the 1920s, when these things were literally unheard-of. The point here is that Dr. Sweet had no problem defending himself at a time when many Blacks still lived in fear of White reprisal for even the slightest deviance from the draconian code of docile submission and compliance imposed on Black behavior.

I would suggest that like Coleman Young, Dr. Ossian Sweet typifies the attitude of Black Detroit even now. This attitude of defiance and refusal to follow the dictates of White authority has also influenced, I would say, the way in which the Pistons were perceived. While many Black people in Detroit embraced this strong sense of Black identity, many Whites found it threatening.

In the early '70s the Pistons still played their home games in Cobo Hall, a venue located in the heart of downtown Detroit. The Pistons even had a Black head coach in Ray Scott, the first African American to win the league's Coach of the Year award. At this time the games were attended by a large number of Black spectators who represented a range of

Black life in the city from the most blue-collar autoworker to the flashiest pimp, and even to the most dignified class of emerging Black professionals. This mix gave Pistons home games a unique character. It was a Black thing, no doubt.

Yet by the late '70s the Pistons had moved way out to the suburb of Pontiac to play in the massive new Silverdome, a football stadium that could be converted to accommodate basketball games. This move to a dome in the 'burbs was consistent with the actions of many other professional sports teams during this time. The Silverdome was never much like a real basketball home, as it was simply too cavernous. But it did replace venerable Cobo Hall as the location for the Pistons, and this meant that a primarily Black sport, bearing the name of a predominantly Black city, was really located in a suburb far away from the team's real home. This contradiction continues to stand out like a sore thumb, to this day. Nonetheless, the Pistons were still informed by the abiding sense of Blackness that emanated from the city of Detroit. And this is what fueled their run in the late '80s, and what made so many people deplore their very existence.

Bad Boys Come Out to Play

The Pistons in the late '80s were a stark departure from the more popular Celtics and Lakers. In an attempt to fashion a distinct identity, the Pistons molded themselves into a strong defensive unit. This was unlike the offensive style that most NBA teams had perfected. Offense was quite visible and quite fun to watch, but defense was not so dramatic. The Pistons brought down the average scores of NBA games substantially during their reign by denying their opponents the opportunity to get good shots and consistently make baskets. Each possession became a frustrating adventure for opposing teams. In addition, the Pistons used their stifling defense as a way to intimidate opponents. Most NBA teams were defined by their offense and would build their teams around offensive-minded players. Yet when forced to play the Pistons, these teams were often unable to match them physically, as this was not a style of ball many teams were suited to play.

In addition to the play of Laimbeer though, the Pistons also had bruising power forward Rick Mahorn, who had been one-half of the infamous "Filthy McNasty" crew with Jeff Ruland when he was with the Washington Bullets. Mahorn, built more like a football player, used his size to his advantage, often knocking opposing players all over the place, or setting them up on a drive and then moving out of the way once the other player got into a rhythm. There is a famous scene of Mahorn knocking Larry Bird down by sticking out his ass that is still funny to look at now. Players who dared go to the basket were often greeted by both Laimbeer and Mahorn, and these shooters would often end up on their ass by the time the play was completed. Laimbeer and Mahorn could frequently be seen laughing after some of these plays, adding insult to injury in a very real way.

See, basketball had been thought of as a finesse sport up until this point. It was often said that, unlike football, basketball was a noncontact sport. Well, the Pistons completely abolished this notion. If you decided to challenge them, particularly in the paint, you would get "touched," as they say, and in no uncertain terms. Many people felt that this style was not the way that basketball should be played, that it was in some manner anathema to the game itself. Unfortunately for them, the Pistons did not care. They were going to play hard regardless of what others said. Indeed, they considered this their calling.

This physical play was important in giving the Pistons a sense of mental domination over their opponents as well. Teams began to fear them, and this the Pistons used to their advantage. There was a notable incident in game seven of the conference finals in 1990, when the Pistons' game face completely intimidated the Chicago Bulls' Scottie Pippen. Though Pippen would go on to great fame over time in his career, he played terribly that day and blamed this poor play on a mysterious migraine headache. Yet many interpreted it as fear and a lack of toughness on his part. Pippen had to overcome this perception before he could live down this incident.

By this point the image of the city of Detroit had violence written all over it. The city had come to be affectionately known as the "Murder Capital." In some cases it was even suggested that Detroit now resembled a Third World city. While many of Detroit's critics and resentful suburbanites embraced this image, many African American residents in the city saw Detroit as uniquely belonging to them and tended to celebrate the prominence and relative power that African Americans enjoyed in a place they could call their own. However, as is often the case, when the Pistons began to contend for a championship, the entire metro area, Black and White, felt a connection to this success.

Because the city was so Black in its population makeup and, more important, in its vibe, many would subtly connect this sensibility to the Pistons and their hard-core style. The Pistons never shied away from this, either. They were a tough, hard-nosed team in a blue-collar city, and this translated to the way they saw themselves and the way that they played when they walked on the court.

Isiah's Comment

What ultimately fueled a great deal of hatred toward the Pistons outside of Detroit were some comments made by Isiah Thomas after the Pistons lost to the Celtics in the 1987 conference finals. Dennis Rodman, a Pistons rookie at the time, had the dubious task of guarding Larry Bird throughout that fateful series. Though Bird and Boston got the best of the Pistons when Isiah threw an errant pass that Bird intercepted and kicked back to Dennis Johnson for the winning basket in game five, the series had been a hard-fought battle, with the Pistons coming oh-so-close to dethroning the mighty Celtics. They would accomplish their mission one year later, with the heartbreak of the '87 loss serving as motivation.

After the '87 series ended, though, some reporters went to Rodman, whose anxiety-laced antics had rubbed many people the wrong way already. The reporters asked him how it felt to guard a legend. Rodman blurted out that he thought Bird was overrated, that Bill Russell was the best player in league history, and the only reason Bird received such acclaim was that he was White.

Rodman at the time was an unknown. He was a promising rookie, but that was it. He did not yet have the public image or profile he would gain some years later with his gender-bending performance. No, in 1987, Dennis Rodman was just about a nonentity outside of Piston basketball. So the reporters went over to Isiah Thomas, repeated Rodman's comments, and asked for Isiah's response. They wanted to know if Isiah agreed with what Rodman had said. To their surprise, Isiah cosigned Rodman, saying that he was in full agreement with the controversial comments. With that, the issue was transformed from the comments of a naive rookie into a national sports story, a headline-making drama of the first order.

Considering that Isiah's bad pass had been the turning point in this series, many considered his remarks to be a reflection of "sour grapes" about having lost the series to Bird and the Celtics. Others simply felt that the comments were wrong. Some even suggested that Thomas's comments were racist. Mostly though, the comments prompted a response of surprise and shock that Isiah had the unmitigated gall to criticize the "great White hope" himself, whose greatness was thought to be indisputable.

Isiah suggested that Bird was overrated and pointed out that if he were Black, he would be thought of as "just another good guy." While the Bird comment may have seemed like blasphemy to many White sportswriters and fans, to many Black people Isiah was simply "telling it like it is" and, in hip hop parlance, "keepin' it real," here speaking the truth regardless of the circumstances or consequences.

Throughout Bird's reign, many Black followers of the game speculated aloud whether the celebration of Bird was exaggerated because of his race. Isiah simply voiced what had been said in Black homes throughout America for some time. Yet there was a media firestorm now, and Isiah was in the center of it: How dare he use the name of "god" in vain like that?

The intensity got to be so strong that Isiah eventually had to hold a press conference to downplay his comments by suggesting that he was joking when he made them. He was forced to cop out and eventually had to endure a public grilling from a hostile Brent Musburger, the CBS announcer, during the NBA finals. Isiah had sinned, and he would have to repent for these sins in public for the rest of his career. This transgression also helped fuel animosity toward the Pistons in the future.

One cannot deny that Larry Bird was a great player. He excelled and so did his team for a significant number of years. My point has always been that Bird did not contribute anything to the game of basketball that was not already there when he arrived. He played excellent basketball for years, but he was not an innovator nor did he transform the game. Bird's public embrace though is very similar to an old Richard Pryor joke regarding the boxer Rocky Marciano. Pryor suggested that it was easy to be good when an entire nation of White people was holding you up, implying that the overwhelming public support and interest that Marciano received helped propel him to his status as heavyweight champion. Bird too benefited a great deal from the support of a public acutely interested in seeing him succeed as a White player in what was otherwise thought to be a Black game.

The real problem that Isiah created with his comment was that he dared articulate a situation that suggested White privilege. The discourse surrounding Bird was that he was a White player valiantly overcoming all sorts of preceived obstacles in his quest to compete with the assumed-to-be-more-physically-gifted Black players who seemed born to play the game. Isiah's comment and others of this sort were simply unheard-of in these heady days of Reaganomics.

Thus Isiah's comments met head-on with a society still bent on believing that there was such a thing as reverse discrimination in the post-Bakke era. Maybe more than any other single act, Isiah's comment helped paint the Pistons as an outlaw band of Black players from a city with a tattered reputation who had a penchant for making basketball, an otherwise innocuous sport, into a racial thing. This was thought to be playing the so-called "race card" to the hilt. When you consider that very few professional athletes say anything now, other than articulating a series of programmed clichéd responses, it becomes even more apparent that Isiah's comments were a shock to the mainstream White system in terms of the sheer honesty embedded in his words.

———

THE INDELIBLE IMAGE created by Isiah's remarks notwithstanding, the act that set the Pistons legacy in stone would come in 1991, at the end of their reign, when they finally lost to the Chicago Bulls in the Eastern Conference finals. The Pistons and the Bulls had met in the playoffs every year between 1988 and 1991, with the Pistons emerging victorious in the first three meetings. This rivalry gained intensity with each year. The Pistons were the dominant team, but the Bulls would close the gap each year, causing many to speculate that Michael Jordan and his emerging team would eventually overcome their nemesis. In 1991 the Bulls finally prevailed, and they did so in style, sweeping the Pistons in four games and leaving no question as to who now had the upper hand.

With the series all but locked up, the Pistons decided not to take their beating quietly and instead went about showcasing their "bad boy" persona one last time. At one point in the game, the Pistons' Dennis Rodman, his hair yet to be dyed, aggressively shoved Scottie Pippen in the back, nearly knocking him into the padded support that holds up the basket. With Pippen already suffering from the "soft" reputation, as a result of the migraine headache excuse from the previous year, this forceful shove by Rodman was designed to send the Bulls scurrying to the exits once again. This time it did not work, though the shove did set the tone and established that the Pistons were not going to go in silence. They were going to go out the same way that they had come in: pushing, shoving, kicking, and letting it be known that they did not give a fuck about what others might have to say about their "thuggish ruggish" style.

When the outcome of the game is clear, late in the fourth quarter, teams customarily pull their starters out. The Bulls had dominated this one almost from the outset, and thus it was obvious who would win well before the final buzzer sounded. So with some time still left on the clock, the Piston starters, led by Isiah and Laimbeer, walked off the court into the locker room, right past the Bulls bench, right in front of Jordan, refusing to engage in the customary postgame handshake.

Sports has always been considered a gentlemanly pursuit, where individuals locked in battle are supposed to shake hands after the contest is over to congratulate the victors and to show that there are no hard feelings. In the hard-fought battles that the Pistons and Bulls had engaged in over the years, however, there was by the end a high degree of animus between the two teams. For starters Michael Jordan had long felt that Isiah was the culprit behind the freeze-out in the 1985 All-Star Game. And the many physically challenging games that the two teams had played did nothing to heal wounds already deeply inflicted. The close proximity of the two cities did not help matters either. Detroit has always felt itself relegated to the shadow that Chicago cast over the rest of the Midwest. This perceived sense of inferiority or justified resentment—however you see it—certainly played a part in this rivalry.

The Pistons felt disrespected. They felt that they were never considered true champions in the way that the Celtics or the Lakers had been. Detroit also felt ignored and cast aside by the league itself, considering that the Pistons' defensive-minded ways were not to the liking of the television networks, not to mention that everyone was waiting to see Michael Jordan on center stage. In the end, this was about respect. The Pistons wanted the respect that went along with being two-time, back-to-back champions. But they felt that the Bulls and Jordan, who at this time had not won anything, were getting all the love that they, the Pistons, never received. So when they walked off the court, they were sending a message that said collectively, "We don't give a fuck!"

Gangsta Lean

Unlike others who could not wait to chide the Pistons for their conduct, I found this walkoff indicative of the dominant aesthetic that had started to inform Blackness around the same time that the Pistons started their championship run in the late '80s. This aesthetic was known as gangsta rap.

The group N.W.A. started to receive a great deal of attention for their incendiary lyrics after their song "Fuck the Police" prompted an FBI memo threatening to take action against the group for inciting violence toward law enforcement. What was significant about N.W.A. was the fact that they expressed a sensibility deeply rooted in the gang culture of Southern California. Their penchant for khakis, flags, skullcaps, and outward rage symbolized the defiant Black youth who had been raised under the extreme conditions imposed by the Reagan era and who had decided to exist on their own terms. In this, they glorified their gang lifestyle for all to see and they embraced the threatening aspects of their persona as opposed to shying away from them. It was as though they said, "Yeah, we're gangstas, so what?!"

Following the success of N.W.A., many other acts emerged that would follow in their footsteps. Being hard, irreverent, and defiant now had a cultural reference point, and this in turn began to pop up throughout all other elements of the culture. Therefore one can read the Pistons' act as one of defiance also. Instead of being held to the tenets of some arbitrary standard of decorum, the Pistons were saying that they would remain committed to being hard: "Not only are we *not* going to shake your hand, we're going to walk right past you so that you know we don't care! Fuck you!" This was the way of the street, in full effect.

The league, the media, and many fans began to strongly criticize the Pistons for what they considered to be disrespect. People began yelling that the walkoff lacked class. Many people felt that when the first Dream Team was formed to play in the 1992 Olympics, that Isiah Thomas was left off the squad as punishment for his past transgressions, especially those involving Michael Jordan, with this famous walk of disrespect heading the list.

At this point, after Magic was forced to retire due to contracting the HIV virus and Larry Bird was starting to fade due to back problems, Jordan had fully emerged as the star of the league. Having defeated Magic and the Lakers in the 1991 finals, and then coming back to beat Portland in 1992 with a barrage of three-point shots in the first game that set the tone for the rest of the series, Jordan was the NBA's center of attention. Jordan had worked so hard to finally overcome the Pistons that in the process the rivalry between him and Isiah seemed to reach epic proportions. Therefore, many speculated that Jordan was the reason that Isiah had been curiously left off the team. Though this was never proven, Jordan did very little to discourage this thought. It was also rumored that Isiah's former general manager, Jack McClosky, and his coach Chuck Daly, who also headed the Dream Team, were not interested in having Isiah on the team either and did not speak up in his favor.

What actually happened remains a mystery. But whatever the reasons, Isiah's absence was a glaring omission. In my mind, Isiah Thomas is the best "little man" to ever play the game. Though some others could lay claim to the title, such as Nate "Tiny" Archibald, who once led the league in scoring and assists in the same year, Isiah remains a better overall choice in my view.

Allen Iverson has the talent to have an outstanding career also, and he seems poised to challenge Isiah's significance if things continue in a positive direction, but at this point Isiah still holds his own. Isiah came into the league as a spectacular point guard with a flair for the dramatic, focused his early sights on dominating the All-Star Game, and could have simply coasted off of this. Yet that was not enough. Isiah demonstrated his ability to take over a game at any time, and in so doing he often reduced bigger men down to his size.

There are many examples of Isiah's desire to win and dominate a game, but two examples stand out in my mind. The first took place in a 1987 playoff game against his childhood friend Doc Rivers and the Atlanta Hawks. The Hawks were the favored team in this series, but the Pistons upset them and went on to the conference finals against the Boston Celtics for the first time. In a crucial third-quarter stretch, Isiah caught fire and began dominating the game like he had done in that ninety-four-second, sixteen-point flurry back in the '84 playoffs. At one point Isiah was so into a groove that, as he walked the ball up the court while being closely guarded by his homey Doc Rivers, he began switching hands and dribbling the ball between his legs. Isiah always had a great "handle," as they say, an amazing ability to dribble the basketball. He appropriated this from the great Harlem Globetrotter legend Marques Haynes, arguably the best ball handler ever. Well, Isiah was switching hands, dribbling between his legs, walking the ball up, and talking "shit" to Doc Rivers all at the same time. It was an amazing sight. Doc was spellbound, and there was nothing he could do but be humiliated. Isiah scored twenty-five points in that quarter alone and went on to lead the Pistons to a victory in that series.

The second example is one that will forever define Isiah's drive as a basketball player. In game six of the 1988 NBA finals the Pistons were battling the Lakers for their first crown. With a three games to two lead, the Pistons were trying to wrap up the series in LA. Again in the third quarter of that game, Isiah would add to his legacy in a major way. At a certain point in the quarter, Isiah sprained his ankle. He was visibly shaken and hurt as he pounded the floor in frustration. His chances for an NBA crown seemed to be slipping away. But he would not give in just yet. Suddenly Isiah began scoring like crazy. He was being guarded by Michael Cooper, a player known as one of the best defensive players in the league. Yet, Isiah was oblivious to Cooper. He scored at will. His ankle was hurting so badly, you could see him limping, hopping even, back up the court on defense. But whenever he got the ball on offense, he did one amazing thing after the other. At a certain point he put the ball up somewhat off balance with one hand and literally hopped backward on one leg to balance himself, and he didn't fall down, either. The ball dropped and Cooper was left to stand there, looking completely defenseless. This image is one that attests to Isiah's ability to be the smallest man on the floor but possess the biggest heart. He scored twenty-five in that quarter, though the surprising Pistons could not win the game or the series with Isiah being injured the rest of the way.

Many people dwell on Isiah's seemingly aimless pass that was stolen by Larry Bird in 1987. Isiah learned from this mistake though and eventually took his team to back-to-back championships. To do so he was required to suppress his own individual goals in order to lead a stronger team, making the other players better. Isiah, the ultimate individual superstar at one point in his career, had, for the betterment of his squad, become the consummate leader, doing what was necessary in order for his team to win as a unit.

This professional sacrifice would normally be celebrated in sports circles where people are always complaining about individuals ignoring the team concept. This was not the case with Isiah. After winning the second championship in 1990, Isiah returned to Detroit to allegations of being involved in a gambling scandal. It seems that some of his checks, for large sums of money, had been found among the checks of one of his neighbors, who was the target of a gambling probe. Isiah said that the neighbor, who owned a grocery store, had agreed to cash the checks for him as a favor so that he would not have to go to the bank. Others suggested that the checks were proof that Isiah was involved in a high-stakes gambling operation. Rumors persisted, but Isiah was never charged with any wrongdoing.

Isiah Thomas is probably one of the most hated players in NBA history. This hatred comes from his leadership role with those "Bad Boy" teams. Unlike the hugely popular Magic or Bird who preceded him, or the most visible icon of the latter half of the twentieth century, Jordan, who came along afterward and rose to prominence, Isiah proved to be a bit less fortunate in terms of the way people felt about him. Though early in his career he was seen as a baby-faced youngster with a disarming smile, by the end that smile was often thought to be a ruse, hiding an evil, sinister heart and masking ill intentions.

People's perception of Isiah seemed to change after his comments about Larry Bird. No longer was he the darling of the league, the little man trying to make it in a big man's game; now he was perceived to be an "evil little muthafucka" who would cut your heart out, given the opportunity. Former teammate Sidney Green, who had a "beef" with Isiah during his short-lived stint with the Pistons, once alluded to the Bird comments as indicative of Isiah's character following an altercation with Isiah.

He was often known in Detroit as a control freak who wanted to micromanage every aspect of the Pistons team. Similar suggestions would be made about Jordan and his team, for instance, but unlike Isiah, with Jordan this micromanaging was often thought of as indicating his commitment to winning. There are rumors that Isiah and Chuck Daly had many disagreements, that he and team general manager Jack McClosky hated each other, and that many of his teammates walked on eggshells around him for fear of incurring his wrath.

As an example of this, observers point to the case of Adrian Dantley. When it was suspected that Isiah engineered the trade in 1989 that sent the veteran Dantley to Dallas for Isiah's close friend Mark Aguirre, many people were quite upset, especially Dantley. Adrian Dantley, or "AD" as he was often called, had become a beloved figure in Detroit, especially after he led the opening game rout of the Lakers in the 1988 finals. Yet it is rumored that he and Isiah had trouble together, and when the trade was made for Isiah's friend, many people cried foul.

When Isiah and his team decided that aggressive physical play would define their existence, and when they continually put Michael Jordan on his ass for all those years, Isiah was insuring that he would never be accorded the acclaim that his play deserved. Being left off the Dream Team was punishment for all his past sins, and being ignored in the minds of many when discussing the true NBA legends is his eternal damnation. Sure, he was selected to the Hall of Fame, sure he was named one of the fifty greatest players ever, and this is all well deserved, but he has never been loved and admired among the real elite, and he deserves to be.

Finally, for all of Isiah's accomplishments in Detroit, it is Joe Dumars who has received all the praise and love of the fans and the Pistons organization. As evidence, it is Dumars, not Isiah, who is now the team's President of Basketball Operations. Dumars was thought to be one of the few Pistons who was not a "Bad Boy." He was one Detroit player who went over to Michael Jordan and shook his hand after that game in 1991. His quiet, low-key persona endeared him to the fans, the league, and obviously the Piston organization, which has entrusted their future to Dumars.

———

AT THE END OF THE DAY the Pistons were a very good basketball team that was never accorded the proper acclaim because they did not fit the image most desired by the league, the television networks, and many of the fans. They were a team that represented a strong, Black—even violent—image, and this was something that had never been seen in the league before. The Boston teams in the '80s were always thought to be "tough" because they played so physically. In the case of the Celtics this was a compliment, not a criticism. But when the Pistons displayed the same style, they were linked to the violent image of Black masculinity being plastered all over the news media as well as the equally notorious image of Detroit itself. The players were unapologetic, however. Indeed, they embraced their negative image and wore their scarlet letter like a Bad Boy badge of honor.

Their rise to prominence was concurrent with the rise of gangsta rap, a genre of music that embraced this thug-life imagery, as opposed to running from it. There were now individuals who had no problem being thought of as gangstas. They probably appreciated this designation as emblematic of their hardened stance against the forces of conformity. Considering all of this, the Pistons were to basketball what gangsta rap was to music; a reality check that clearly spelled out what was really going on. Basketball was a Black man's game and a street game at that. The Pistons helped usher this sensibility into basketball and in doing so they pushed forward the modern evolution of the game.

This urban sensibility had begun to define virtually all of professional basketball. The Pistons were an urban menace. There was no finesse, no grace, no attempt at playing to a shallow sense of gentility either. Just good, hard-nosed basketball with a dose of gangsterism thrown in for good measure.

The Takeover
The Fab Five, Hip Hop, and College 'Ball

THE HEART OF THE CITY

By the late 1980s professional basketball had most defiantly embraced the urban aesthetic. With the physical decline of Larry Bird, the league's last truly great White American player, the streetball style that had been detested by so many had come to define the game itself. Though Utah's John Stockton would gain a great deal of attention and support, he was in no way the player that Bird was, and playing in Utah made him even less visible. Certainly the league's best player, Michael Jordan, was a guy capable of doing it fundamentally, fusing what I have always called "the formal and the vernacular," and this is what gave him his unique edge. More often than not, though, Jordan's street game took over.

When the Chicago Bulls went up against the Portland Trail Blazers in the 1992 NBA finals, Michael's biggest challenge was supposed to come from the Blazers' Clyde Drexler. Clyde "The Glide" had been a star in college at the University of Houston and an integral part of the Phi Slamma Jamma crew that also included Hakeem Olajuwan. Many people at the time suggested that Clyde was as good as Jordan. But by being in a small market like Portland, he did not get the proper media attention. Thus few people knew how good he really was.

The point is, Jordan's chief competition was someone known for "gliding" to the basket, another example of the prevalence of the urban aesthetic in the game. Many of the game's up-and-coming young players also pledged allegiance to this potentially exciting street style as well: Gary Payton, Larry Johnson, Tim Hardaway, and Derrick Coleman, to name just a few. Though the visibility of the street aesthetic would in coming years completely dominate almost every aspect of basketball, in the early '90s it was already clear that this aesthetic had won the style wars and was in place to stay.

Big Man on Campus

This was not the case though in the game of college basketball. Whereas professional basketball was indeed a player's league, and the wide-open style being played was one where the athletic ability of the players took precedence, college was still controlled by the college presidents, administrators, and especially the coaches. In the pros a coach could be fired if he did not get along with his star player, but in college a star player could be dismissed quickly if he did not act in accordance with the coach. Why, even Larry Bird was booted from the Indiana University team when he could not come to terms with Bobby Knight's military ways. College was where you had to get with the program, literally, or you were out.

Coaches in college ball were often like gods in their own right. The coaches who won consistently, like a Dean Smith, for instance, had become institutions at their respective universities. Considering that players would come and go every four years, coaches were the permanent stabilizing force. Teams were often built around their coach's personality, and entire programs tended to be evaluated more so than individual players. In this regard, three distinct programs were prominent in early '90s college basketball circles, and these three programs, Duke, UNLV, and Michigan, illustrate the changing dynamics of the game itself. College basketball had become a big-money operation, and the image of each respective school was often tied directly to the visibility of its basketball team on national television. The early '90s were a turning point in the way that college basketball would function, relative to its ability to represent issues of race, class, and style.

———

THE STATE OF NORTH CAROLINA in the early to mid-'80s was college basketball central. The University of North Carolina under Dean Smith had been to the NCAA finals twice, in '81 and '82, and had won a dramatic championship game against Georgetown in '82 when a freshman named Michael Jordan hit what turned out to be the game-winning shot. One year later the surprising North Carolina State team shocked the world with a stunning upset of the heavily favored University of Houston Cougars with their high-flying Phi Slamma Jamma offensive assault. With that victory, NC State, under coach Jim Valvano, suggested that UNC could no longer claim exclusive rights to that contested ACC territory with their victory. Yet at the school that was soon to become the center of the college basketball world, Duke, Mike Krzyzewski, better known as "Coach K," was only a few years into his tenure.

Coach K was a disciple of Bobby Knight, having been Knight's assistant while at the United States Military Academy at West Point. Though he had just come to Duke in the early '80s, K was already in the NCAA championship game by 1986. He lost in a close game to Louisville. Yet this was just the beginning. Duke would advance to the Final Four seven times between 1986 and 1994, winning back-to-back championships in '91 and '92. By then Duke had become the best program in college basketball.

There was a lull for a few years in the mid-90s. During 1994–95, Coach K sat out most of the season due to back problems, though some would suggest it was to maintain his stellar coaching record in light of having a bad team that year. After this brief hiatus, Duke was back winning again in the late '90s, going to the finals in 1999, 2001, and 2002, winning another title in 2001. In light of this success, Coach K was often compared to the great UCLA coach of old, John Wooden.

What was startling about Duke's success in the early years of K's tenure was the fact that his teams tended to be predominantly White in an age when basketball was increasingly being viewed as a Black sport.

Though the first Duke team that made it to the championship game in 1986 featured Johnny Dawkins as the star and future coaching prodigy Tommy Amaker in the starting backcourt, these two were the only Black players of any real significance on that team. There would not be another prominent Black player on a Duke team until Grant Hill arrived in the early '90s. Duke would often feature one or two athletic Black players, a David Henderson here, a Robert Brickey there, but no real standout Black stars like the ones who filled the rosters of the other college teams.

What made this lack of a Black presence even more compelling was the fact that Duke University is considered one of the nation's elite universities, and it is arguably the best university in the South. It is a private school that boasts some of the most selective admissions policies around. Duke was thought to be the epitome of Southern gentility, and the success of the basketball team in the late '80s/early '90s seemed to underscore some of the same sugarcoated ideas about racial harmony that were being represented in films like *Driving Miss Daisy*.

Duke is not the kind of university that normally dominates in college sports. No, this is not some large state school, some basketball factory, drawing on the resources surrounding it. Instead it is a small, private, elite Southern university with a stellar academic reputation. It would seem then, by implication, that maybe Black players did not belong or could not gain admission if they wanted to.

The White players at Duke, like many of the White students, tended to come from a middle- or upper-middle-class background. There was a distinct aura of privilege when this team took the floor. For instance, one of their stars in the mid to late '80s was the overrated Danny Ferry, son of an NBA general manager. Duke's lily-White teams stood out when contrasted against the predominantly Black teams they would often play against.

Some would suggest that the Duke team gave the impression that they were student-athletes in the truest sense, not some hired hands recruited to play ball who could not pass a college exam if they were given the correct answers. In a time when propositions to change the academic requirements at college athletic programs were being revised and openly debated, Duke seemed to embody the purity of the college game, one where students went to school to study first and play 'ball second. The Blue Devils were a throwback to a previous time in the most positive way.

There were some strong racial politics at work here as well as some issues related to class standing. To recruit a predominantly White team at this point in history was no mere coincidence. This was something that required effort and attention. The Boston Celtics for years drafted practically every player that came out of the overly White Brigham Young University in order to maintain that so-called "Celtic mystique."

Duke appeared to search through every crack and crevice they could find in order to maintain the desired White balance. They would have had to. The fact that the team was so successful with their recruits tended to fuel the fire of perceptions. The implication was that a school could win without having to compromise its reputation as a quality academic institution by bringing in those academically unqualified Black players from the ghetto. Duke seemed to be above reproach here, and its Blue Devils were often regarded as model citizens, celebrated as college basketball icons of all that was good and right with the world.

———

BY THE EARLY '90S, Duke was a regular participant in the Final Four. It was almost expected that the team would reach that lofty plateau each year. The problem was that, even though the Blue Devils had created such high expectations for themselves, they were never able to capture their first championship. For me, success has always been relative. If you are good enough to reach the Final Four every year, at some point this becomes routine. Sure this was an impressive feat. But it makes sense that at some point people might begin to wonder whether Duke had what it took to reach the next level and finally win the whole tournament.

After regular trips to the Final Four in the '80s, Duke still had not won the title by 1990. That year they faced a formidable opponent, the Runnin' Rebels from the University of Nevada at Las Vegas (UNLV). In the championship game, UNLV put Duke to shame, beating them resoundingly by a thirty-point margin, 103–73. The celebrated Duke team, generally regarded as a smart basketball team that played hard and made few mistakes, was on this day a second-rate squad of inferior players that could not do anything right against the more athletic and energetic UNLV squad. It was as though Duke did not even belong on the same floor with UNLV. To make it to a championship game and lose this bad was an embarrassment.

Rebels in the Desert

Unlike Duke, UNLV was not a celebrated team. The Runnin' Rebels were generally regarded as a bunch of outlaws. Jerry Tarkanian had been their coach for many years. During this time he was consistently under scrutiny from the NCAA. Unable to attract big-name players straight out of high school, Tarkanian had long ago started the practice of recruiting junior college transfers. Though "JC transfers" are now a regular part of college 'ball, there was a time when these players were often seen as damaged goods. In addition, Tarkanian's players were often individuals who had emerged from ghetto surroundings and still displayed the trappings of this sometimes rough upbringing in the rarefied and genteel world of college basketball.

One of the players in question was the New York playground legend Lloyd "Sweetpea" Daniels. Tarkanian's recruitment of Daniels led to one of the longest investigations in NCAA history and eventually resulted in Tarkanian resigning as basketball coach. Daniels was involved in several drug deals gone bad that came to light, and he was even a victim of gunplay while traversing this netherworld. He was never actually able to play at UNLV, but his recruitment suggested that the type of players Tarkanian had been going after were not suburban schoolboys.

Tarkanian himself was not a stranger to NCAA inquiries, having originally been investigated by the NCAA while coaching at Long Beach State back in the 1970s. He was the poster boy for what many people felt was wrong with college athletics. He recruited players who were not considered fit for college and who were thought to make a mockery of the notion of "student athlete." The players were seen to be simply using the college game as a minor league system on their way to pro basketball. The many racial stereotypes concerning academically unqualified Black players who came from ghetto environments drove home the point here. Many felt that these Black individuals were "taking away" opportunities from more qualified White students. Armed with this knowledge, it is possible to begin understanding how the renegade image of Tarkanian and his teams came to be the scourge of the image-conscious NCAA.

What is also significant here is the location of the university. In the late 1980s and early '90s Las Vegas was still known as "Sin City." This was well before the repeated image makeovers that the city would undergo throughout the '90s, at one point during these makeovers even being ironically touted a "family" town, a point accentuated at the conclusion of Martin Scorsese's meditation on old Vegas, *Casino* (1995). In the late '80s/early '90s Las Vegas, a city of many transients, was still associated in the public mind with the mafia, gambling, the carousing of the Rat Pack, and all sorts of tawdry endeavors. It was certainly not the kind of place where one would assume that much intellectual activity went on. More important, in distance and in image, Las Vegas was about as far from the idyllic Durham, North Carolina, campus of Duke University as one could ever get.

When UNLV plastered Duke in 1990, many felt sorry for the Blue Devils. Here was this squad that epitomized what college ball was all about, student athletes giving their all for the old team, going against a gang of thuggish semiprofessionals simply waiting for their turn to cash in on the NBA's riches. It was perceived to be "men" against "college boys." In this regard, Duke did not have a chance. Some even suggested that UNLV could have beaten some of the weaker pro teams. So even though Duke had been humiliated on the court, its players were acquitted in the court of public opinion due to the favorable image that they created.

By the NCAA tournament of 1991, UNLV was pursuing a unprecedented run at having an undefeated season. The last team to go a whole season without a loss was the Bobby Knight–led Indiana Hoosiers in 1976. This was a mark that seemed nearly impossible to attain, and yet

UNLV, which returned all of its stars from the previous year, looked poised to do it, with most of its victories being by double-digit margins throughout the season. UNLV had not been challenged at all during the regular season.

Duke also returned a number of players from the previous year. But even though they looked more experienced, the Blue Devils still appeared to be no match for the Runnin' Rebels. The two teams would meet in the Final Four, though this for all intents and purposes was clearly the championship game. UNLV's thirty-point victory the year before seemed to be not that long ago. And so it was thought that even though they might put up a better fight, Duke still really had no chance to win.

The game itself was a dogfight, as they say in sports. Neither team appeared able to take over the game, but Duke surprised many when they pulled off a close victory. UNLV players kept the game close but never really looked to be playing their game. The Rebels' star player, Larry Johnson, was virtually invisible, even nonchalantly declining to take the last shot at the end of the game. Since Duke had been so soundly beaten the year before, it appeared that something was wrong. How could UNLV go from total dominance to losing such a close game, while never really looking like they were in the game anyway? With UNLV ensconced in Las Vegas, many people suggested that the proverbial "fix was in," alleging that Johnson and others had possibly thrown the game. Though this charge was never taken seriously, the loss did seem odd.

This game was a triumph for those who felt that college athletics had gotten out of hand. The Georgetown–Villanova final in 1985 saw a seemingly inferior Villanova team upset defending champion Georgetown, and this was quite similar to the way the Duke/UNLV game unfolded. In both cases, teams with a strong urban style, featuring a number of players who fit the urban mold, were defeated by teams that played fundamental basketball and had a relatively large number of White players.

When you consider that both Georgetown and UNLV were defending champions trying to win a second straight title, their respective losses seem even more shocking. The conclusion after both of these games was that good coaching and determination can defeat arrogant athletic showmanship every time. It was the *Hoosiers* myth writ large once again. Old-school fundamentals had won out over new-school streetball. Mind over matter. The White boys had claimed another victory in the ongoing surrogate race war that basketball had become.

———

DUKE'S STAR PLAYER for those triumphant years was Christian Laettner. An arrogant player if ever there was one, Laettner was instead described as confident. He appeared to be the heir apparent to Larry Bird. Laettner had enjoyed a spectacular career at Duke, highlighted by the last-second turnaround catch-and-shoot jumper that he dropped on Kentucky to help Duke advance to the 1992 final game. He was a big man who could do it all: shoot, play inside or outside, and lead his squad. He seemed all but destined to take over the Great White Hope mantle from Larry Bird once he made it to the pros. As further testament to the regard in which he was held, Laettner was the only college player selected to be a member of the Dream Team in 1992. Laettner's selection was especially suspect considering that Shaquille O'Neal, a standout at LSU during that time and a player who has become the most dominant individual of his generation, would have been the obvious choice.

Laettner's counterpart on the Blue Devils was the undersized Bobby Hurley. Whereas Laettner had a certain style to his game, Hurley was all over the place. He was what sportscasters like to call "scrappy." As a small player, Hurley was seen as an overachiever who pushed beyond his physical limits to excel at a game for which he certainly did not have the size or speed. Hurley was the son of a high school coach from New Jersey, and this also informed his persona as a tough, hard-nosed, intelligent kid who was willing to do whatever it took to win a basketball game.

While both of these players were very good in college, with Laettner being one of the all-time greats of the college game, neither of them enjoyed much distinction playing in the pros. Hurley's undistinguished career was cut short by an auto accident, and Laettner's most memorable moment in the league was being slapped by his teammate at the time, Jerry Stackhouse, during a card game on a team flight. Yet these two players along with Coach K were the face of Duke basketball for several years during their reign on top.

Nigga Neutral

The player who proved to be the best for Duke was younger than either Laettner or Hurley, but had to wait his turn before demonstrating his immense skills. Grant Hill was like a descendant of Bill Cosby's television Huxtable family. His father, Calvin Hill, was a former Dallas Cowboy who had graduated from Yale, and his mother, Janet Hill, was a prominent DC consultant who had been a suitemate of Hillary Clinton's at Wellesley. It would also be appropriate here to suggest that Hill could be compared to another culturally assimilated figure from his generation, the nonthreatening Will Smith. Ironically, Hill was at one time romantically linked to the actress Jada Pinkett, the woman Smith is currently married to.

Grant Hill was the player who threw the picture-perfect pass to Laettner that resulted in the game-winning shot against Kentucky in 1992. Hill was athletic, but he also possessed a great knowledge of the game. And like Michael Jordan, he could play both textbook and streetball. Yet the opportunities to play streetball were few and far between at Duke. Hill, though, had to suppress much of his game until Laettner and Hurley left Duke.

Once he arrived in the league in 1994, Hill was immediately touted as another in a long line of players thought to be the next Michael. As the league got younger and the contests became more and more of a showcase for players nurtured in the street game, and as the influence of hip hop culture expanded, there was a desire to see someone fill the shoes that Michael had worn so well. Jordan abruptly decided to sit out for a season and a half in the mid-90s. When this happened, the absence of a true successor was obvious. Grant Hill, though only a rookie, was anointed to fill this role.

Hill's impressive pedigree was augmented by the fact that he also embodied a non–hip hop demeanor. In a league where the predominance of Black players was now a given, Hill's upper-middle-class status gave him an edge over his lower-class brethren. Though he was not White, he was the functional equivalent in a world where class had come to supplant race as the prevailing norm in determining cultural identity. *GQ* magazine even had the audacity to put Hill on the cover and pose the loaded question, "Can Grant Hill Save Sports?" Save sports from what, one might ask? Well, of course, "save" here referred to saving sports from the emerging and threatening influence of hip hop culture.

In a basketball world where the question of race has been normalized, where Blackness is front and center, those defined otherwise would be individuals who defy the assumed class distinction of being from the 'hood. Grant Hill, an upper-middle-class Black man, was much easier to deal with than some of the other players in the league who hailed from the bottom rung of America's social and economic ladder. In many ways Grant Hill ushered in a time in the NBA when this class issue would come to assume a prominent place in the way that the league was represented.

As the White players in the NBA increasingly came from wartorn landscapes like Bosnia, Croatia, or some of the newly formed republics of the former Soviet Union, White American players became the true minority. Class became the most useful way of distinguishing Black players, who were now the majority population, by far. What made this unusual, though, was the fact that basketball was one of the only places in society where Blackness was the norm and Black people were in the majority. Therefore basketball by the mid-'90s became a site where race and class distinctions were quite prevalent and ultimately functioned very differently than they did anywhere else.

A Brand-New Flava

With the upset of UNLV in the 1991 Final Four, Duke had avenged an embarrassing loss from the year before, and the Blue Devils had also made it clear that, at least in college basketball, there was still room for tradition and, some would even suggest, virtue. Duke's victory was seen as good triumphing over evil, as right prevailing over wrong. The issue of race and class permeated this thinking.

In the case of UNLV, it was Duke's upper-class elite Whiteness against the Rebels' ghetto. Yet Duke's opponent in the 1992 finals, the University of Michigan Wolverines, offered a different sense of Blackness and challenged Duke for attention in a unique way.

When Michigan announced its new recruiting class in 1991, mouths hung open all over the college basketball world. By way of background, college coaches often fall into one of two categories. There are those coaches who are praised for their ability to coach on the floor, and then there are those who are celebrated as great recruiters. On occasion, there are coaches who do both with equal precision.

Dean Smith is arguably one of the greatest recruiters ever, having sent star after star to the NBA. Yet Smith's teams were often under-achievers when competing in the NCAA tournament, losing numerous times when they were the favored team. Smith in his long tenure at UNC won only two NCAA championships. On the other hand, he has coached great players like Bob McAdoo, Walter Davis, James Worthy, Sam Perkins, Kenny Smith, Rasheed Wallace, Jerry Stackhouse, and Vince Carter, players who all enjoyed successful pro careers, as well as the greatest of them all, Michael Jordan. Smith was such a good recruiter that eventually he did not even really have to recruit. Players wanted to come to North Carolina so badly that Dean could pick and choose whom he wanted.

Coach K on the other hand was never a great recruiter, though his most recent teams have suggested a concerted effort in recruiting the top blue-chip players from around the country. K tended to go after players who fit his mold and who could play his style of basketball. Most of them never amounted to much as pro players, but they tended to prevail in college because they fit into the Duke system.

Michigan provided an interesting contrast to both Duke and North Carolina. In 1989, Michigan won the NCAA tournament. Michigan consistently put strong teams on the floor, going back to the days of Johnny Orr in the '70s. In the 1980s their coach, Bill Frieder, proved to be one of the best recruiters in the country, mining the basketball-rich vaults of nearby Detroit and Flint, Michigan, using the school's influence all over the football-minded Midwest to attract the best players. Frieder, though, was a terrible game coach, and his inability to make much use of his spectacular talent had become legendary.

Right before the 1989 NCAA tournament started, Frieder announced that he would be leaving Michigan at the conclusion of the tournament for a new gig at Arizona State. Michigan's athletic director at the time, the dictatorial Bo Schembechler, a celebrated Michigan football coach who had been promoted to running the school's vast athletic program, was not having any of it. Schembechler emphatically stated that he wanted a "Michigan man" coaching the basketball team during the tournament, and promptly relieved Frieder of his duties. Michigan assistant Steve Fisher was named "interim" coach and given the immediate task of running the program through the NCAA tournament. In the off-season, Schembechler said, Michigan would go after a prominent coach to fill the vacated Frieder position.

Michigan, a team thought to be in disarray, astonishingly used this opportunity to go on a tear through the NCAA tournament and ended up surprising everyone when they defeated Seton Hall for the 1989 championship. Fisher eventually had the "interim" removed from his title and was named head coach shortly after the tournament ended.

What else could Michigan do? Here was a man, Fisher, who had taken a team that looked to be totally disorganized and on the verge of collapse and turned it into a champion squad over a three-week period. Whereas Frieder was always criticized for his inability to get the best out of the incredible players he recruited, Fisher had in no time flat turned these underachievers into winners. Michigan had to hire the man full-time. It would have been unthinkable not to.

Before the 1991 season, Fisher announced that he had signed five of the best players in the country. There were high school all-Americans

Chris Webber and Jalen Rose from Detroit, Juwan Howard from Chicago, and Ray Jackson and Jimmy King from Texas. This was a spectacular group of players, who looked to lead Michigan for years to come. Though they would be only freshmen, the excitement was high around the Ann Arbor campus because it seemed that the Wolverines were destined for glory. It did not take long for the glory to begin either, as Fisher decided early in the season to start all five of the freshman players at the same time.

College basketball works on a system where experience is valued. Juniors and seniors are celebrated. They are thought to have earned their place in the starting lineup after having paid their dues as underclassmen. There are exceptions, of course, and particularly exceptional freshmen can make an immediate impact, as Jordan did at UNC. But five freshmen at the same time? This was unheard-of.

The only time a team might start five freshmen would be in a rebuilding year, when they did not have a choice. No one would expect much at all from a squad like this. This would be a coach's worst nightmare. The relative inexperience of an all-freshman starting lineup would suggest that the team in question would be in for a long season of losses and disappointments. But Steve Fisher turned perceived disappointment into opportunity and virtue. Michigan's starting five, all freshmen, were so good that people began calling them "the Fab Five."

Michigan's five freshmen were not only a novelty, they were a very good basketball team. They eventually advanced all the way to the 1992 NCAA finals, losing to the more experienced Duke team but making a name for themselves in the process. Michigan had confounded all conventional wisdom regarding experience in college basketball. No longer was it guaranteed that a more experienced team would defeat one with lesser experience, because even though Michigan lost to Duke in the finals, they had to defeat several other more experienced teams in the process.

In the past, a team could draw criticism for starting one freshman player. As a matter of fact, freshmen had been allowed to participate in the NCAA only since 1972. Now here were five freshmen who were born in the immediate aftermath of this NCAA rule change, and they had advanced all the way to the championship game. This was nothing short of amazing.

Michigan's prominence made the Fab Five one of the most interesting stories in sports. With the Wolverines on national television all the time, the Fab Five received a great deal of attention. They were young, exciting, and certainly a joy to watch. Five freshmen who played with so much poise, so much confidence, along with the requisite youthful swagger, made these young 'ballers the talk of college basketball.

Michigan, a university that enjoys a stellar academic reputation, was one of the most highly regarded public institutions in the country, and their legendary sports programs made it one of the premier places to play. When the Fab Five all decided to attend the university, people suspected that maybe in a year or two this bunch might blossom into something special, but certainly not as fast as they did.

Michigan's most visible player was Chris Webber, who had attended the elite private high school Country Day in the Detroit suburb of Birmingham. Webber was from the city but had been recruited to attend Country Day and became one of the best players in the nation. He possessed the unique ability to walk both sides of the street, if you will, having been raised in Detroit, but now having the social and academic experience that only an elite private school like Country Day could provide. His counterpart was all Detroit though. Jalen Rose was a graduate of Detroit's Southwestern High School, and he had the playground game and the style to match. Webber and Rose, both hailing from Detroit, were the faces of this most visible team.

All of the Fab Five had been born in the early 1970s and grew up in the 1980s. They came of age at a time when hip hop was the music that had the deepest impact on Black youth. Long before hip hop was popular to the masses, it was quite significant as a cultural form to young African Americans. Those members of the Fab Five were at the forefront of a generation for whom hip hop was the soundtrack of their lives. Therefore when the Fab Five took the court in the early '90s, their connection to hip hop culture was on display for all to see.

Michael Jordan had early on shaved off his hair, to camouflage a receding hairline. This practical matter had become a style statement, however, as Michael's influence began spreading like wildfire. When members of the Fab Five, en masse, decided to sport the same style, the "baldie" became the look of choice for young Black men all over the country. You could see this style on display when watching the increasingly abundant hip hop videos broadcast regularly on MTV, and on the basketball court as well.

In addition, Jordan would always wear his basketball shorts longer than normal, to cover up the North Carolina practice shorts that he wore underneath. This, too, became a style statement. The Fab Five began wearing their shorts long also, even adding a few more inches to the length at which Jordan wore his. Their shorts were also quite baggy. Jalen Rose, who was pretty skinny, epitomized this new look with the long, baggy shorts that were, in hip hop parlance, "saggin'." The length we can attribute to Jordan, but the baggy part we can link with the penitentiary. Prisoners, prohibited from wearing belts, were forced to wear pants that sagged and were slung low on their asses. By the early '90s, prison chic was starting to dominate hip hop fashion as the prevalence of gangsta rap became more evident.

The hip hop culture emerging from the West Coast in the late '80s and early '90s was directly connected to gang life in LA, and the penitentiary was a central location in this narrative. Saggin' became a popular way of wearing pants—loose-fitting, hung low on the waist, and in many cases revealing one's underwear. As Black fashion designers, such as the creators of the Cross Colors label, started to receive some visibility in the early '90s, this baggy style became a staple.

It was thought that most clothes available off the rack were cut for a White body type. Jeans, for instance, were too narrow in the seat. So these Black clothing designers began making clothes in accordance with a Black body type, and this is when this baggy style really became a common component of hip hop fashion. The Fab Five took it to the court. With the visibility they had, this style was on display for all to see. This style was also strikingly different from the more traditional short, skimpy, and tight basketball shorts of old that, when looking back at archival footage, seem like hot pants.

The members of the Fab Five were young, and their youthful energy was expressed not only in their style, but also in the energy that they exerted on the court. They also engaged in a great deal of shit-talking on the floor, in keeping with the street-game tradition. This brashness was quite a departure from the more traditional demeanor that college players were supposed to display. Their coach, Steve Fisher, let them play and put few restraints on their behavior. This freedom of expression made for an interesting and compelling cultural force that went far beyond the game of college basketball. The Fab Five were an attraction. They were more akin to hip hop stars than they were to basketball players.

With the success of the Fab Five, Michigan apparel began selling like crazy at athletic apparel stores all over the country. University of Michigan basketball jerseys could be seen in places far away from the Ann Arbor campus. Nike had a contract to make Michigan's uniforms, and they began selling replica versions of them to the public. With the exception of North Carolina apparel, which was directly connected to the popularity of Jordan, Michigan "gear" was the most popular on the streets and in the suburbs.

In short order this Michigan apparel became synonymous with being hip. It started a major hip hop style trend that involved wearing athletic jerseys as a fashion staple as opposed to simply being another way of displaying pride in one's favorite team. All of this is something we can easily attribute to the prevailing influence of the Fab Five.

The Fab Five embodied a new style that was already in place on the streets, but was now available for mainstream consumption. They were the first *hip hop team*. Their youthful expression, their brash ways, what in hip hop would be referred to as their "steelo" or "steez," was such that it caught the more conservative elements of college basketball off guard.

Though the Fab Five made it to the championship game in '92 and '93, they lost both games. The second of these two games was botched by the now-infamous "time-out" that Chris Webber called when Michigan had none left. Yet they did set the game and the culture on its ear by accomplishing so much at such an early age. For a team of five freshmen to make it to the finals is amazing in and of itself. To follow this up the second year proved that it was no fluke.

Ultimately however, their inexperience worked against their winning a championship. But their significance was way beyond college basketball at this point. They were the team that brought hip hop and basketball together in a way that no one before had done, and in a way that would influence basketball from that point forward.

After that fateful time-out, Chris Webber decided to forfeit the last two years of his college basketball eligibility and turn pro. This effectively ended the Fab Five's reign. Webber went on to play for the Golden State Warriors and he had an incredible first season, winning the coveted Rookie of the Year award. At the beginning of his second season, though, Webber and Warriors coach Don Nelson butted heads, and the Warriors traded Webber to Washington.

Nelson, an old-school coach and a former member of the Boston Celtics, felt that Webber should go through a customary hazing period that NBA rookies were supposed to endure as part of the tradition. Webber, now a multimillionaire, felt that he was above this demeaning behavior and refused to be subjected to it. This, for Nelson, was too arrogant. Webber rejected this military-like dictate and instead asserted the fact that his income and his ability as a basketball player made him immune to such treatment.

This attitude, this dismissal of tradition in favor of one's own sense of self-determination and identity, was again straight out of the hip hop world. It was a world that intentionally created distance between itself and previous generations. Nelson's old-school military style was supplanted by Webber's new-school hip hop aesthetic, and this resulted in Webber being traded and labeled a "head case." Webber became the poster child for what was wrong with the new breed of NBA players, and his reputation suffered for a long time due to this cultural misunderstanding and expansive generation gap.

———

THE TRANSITION FROM UNLV to Duke to the Fab Five of Michigan is one that reveals the changes taking place in college basketball and the culture at large from the late '80s through the early '90s. While Duke was keeping the flame burning in college for White ballplayers, White Americans increasingly were disappearing from the pros. The Fab Five, on the other hand, turned basketball into an ongoing rap video. Their style was such that it drew attention to the fact that a new influence was circulating through Black culture, and they were the generation to represent it on the court. That cultural influence was, of course, hip hop. Its direct influence on the game of basketball, both in style and in disposition, was now an indisputable part of the game.

The Fab Five had translated hip hop through basketball, and 'ball was one of many vehicles through which hip hop would spread to society at large. Also, like hip hop, the Fab Five became an extremely popular bunch who transcended basketball while being sponsored by it. Their popularity was not confined to only Black people, either. They were hugely popular with many young White fans. This, too, paralleled what was happening in hip hop as the music began to reach the masses. Finally, the Fab Five did not conform. They played their style, wore their saggin' shorts, and rocked the baldie. The players did not try to be anything other than what they were: young Black men from an urban environment who were firmly and without reservation on a hip hop trip.

On July 14, 2003, Chris Webber pleaded guilty to a lesser charge of criminal contempt in connection with what was originally a charge of lying to a federal grand jury about receiving funds from a University of Michigan booster named Ed Martin. Webber had supposedly taken money from Martin from the time he was in high school throughout his time as a student athlete at Michigan. Webber's Fab Five U of M teammate Jalen Rose had already admitted that he took money from Martin in 2002. Michigan then instituted a self-imposed probation and the NCAA imposed their own sanctions on the University's basketball program in response to those incidents with Webber and Rose, and others involving former U of M players. As part of the probation, Michigan had to forfeit all wins and vacate all record of appearances in the NCAA tournament during the Fab Five era. In other words, the Fab Five has been officially written out of U of M history.

Michigan may be able to write them out of history, but they cannot erase the massive influence the Fab Five had on basketball and hip hop culture during their reign in the early '90s. I'll leave the policing to the NCAA and the court system but the Fab Five's legacy remains untouched.

Leaders of the New School
The Answer, "Karaoke Jordan," and the Modern-Day Balla

Your reign on the top was short like leprechauns.
—THE NOTORIOUS B.I.G., "Kick in the Door"

Hiatus

hen the 1993 NBA season concluded, Michael Jordan and the Chicago Bulls had won their third straight championship. They were the first team to "three-peat" in the modern era. Jordan had vanquished all previous demons and seemed poised to continue winning for as long as he decided to play basketball. That seemed to be forever. Then, suddenly, he was gone, just like that, right before our very eyes.

Jordan decided to "retire" before the 1993–94 season began. This shocking announcement left everyone guessing. Why would a man at the top of his game walk away with so much more to give, with so much more basketball to be played? The NBA had coasted now for several years on Jordan's greatness. Jordan was such a bright, shining moment that at times it seemed like there was really no one else in the league. The others simply appeared to be there so that Jordan would have someone to play against. Jordan was the NBA, and it was quite clear at this point in history that his silhouette, no disrespect to Jerry West, should be the one serving as the NBA logo.

In the absence of Jordan, the league now appeared to be quite vulnerable. While Jordan was playing, the league experienced unparalleled growth. The NBA had added four new teams, one each in Charlotte and Miami, and two Canadian franchises, one team in Vancouver and the other in Toronto. Television revenues were way up, and NBA licensed merchandise was flying out of the stores in record numbers. All this happened during the tenure of Michael Jordan. Now with all of this set in motion, the man who had provided the spark was walking away from the game, and the league did not have any other stars remotely able to assume this now visibly empty space. This again prompted a great deal of weeping and gnashing of teeth among league brass, the media, and the public.

What was even more depressing was that with Jordan's retirement, it became obvious that not only were there no superstars in waiting to take Jordan's spot, but the younger generation of ballplayers did not seem to offer any promise of positive change to come either. The same day that Jordan announced that he would leave the game in 1993, Charlotte's Larry Johnson signed the biggest NBA contract ever at that time. As Jordan was saying his farewells, Johnson was signing a check that would make him a wealthy man for years to come. Johnson had been good early on in his career at Charlotte, but far from great. If he was the future, it left a lot to be desired.

Jordan seemed to have it all. He was a great basketball player, a valuable icon, a compelling interview subject, and a strong image for the league and American culture in general. Johnson was at that time defined by his gold teeth and some annoying Converse commercials in which he played a fictional Moms Mabley–like character called "Grandma-ma."

There was no comparison between the two. Jordan was by now a sartorial marvel, always clean and always with the right thing to say. Johnson was a joke, a wannabe, a player who had his image reduced to that of a novelty, a mascot even. If he was an indication of what the league had to look forward to, things were in sad shape.

The league at this point had begun to rely on Jordan. He brought in many people who otherwise would not watch a basketball game, because his status as cultural icon so transcended the game itself. Television ratings were up and interest in basketball was at an all-time high. Jordan's early retirement, then, left a big gaping hole that exposed the league's vulnerability. There was no "air" apparent, no one to fill the celebrated Air Jordan shoes, at least not anyone who would take over right away.

During the year and a half that Jordan sat out, to many the game seemed to deteriorate. Thus, when he returned to the league again in 1995, there was a welcome sigh of relief on the part of all those who bemoaned his early exit, especially league officials. Jordan's return, against Indiana in March 1995, was one of the highest rated television broadcasts of an NBA game in history. Jordan and the Bulls came up short against Orlando in the playoffs that year, and it appeared that maybe he had lost a step. Many wondered whether the time off had perhaps dulled his skills.

By the start of the 1995–96 season, it was clear to all concerned that Jordan had not lost anything at all. The Bulls, who had added the eccentric, gender-bending Dennis Rodman in the off-season, went on to post a league record 72–10 regular season record and eventually won another championship, defeating Seattle in the finals. Not only was Jordan back, but he was back with a vengeance. Having honed a new fadeaway shot while on leave, Jordan—though not nearly as athletic as he had been originally—continued to be an unstoppable force. He was in this way similar to Muhammad Ali.

When Ali first began making his mark on boxing in the early 1960s, he was quite fast and used his footwork, hand speed, and overall quickness to defeat opponents. Yet after a protracted layoff due to his legal problems arising from his decision not to go to Vietnam, he returned in the 1970s an older man, no longer able to rely on his superior athletic gifts alone. When watching Ali's now legendary fight against George Foreman in 1974, it is obvious that he had lost a few steps, if not many steps. Nonetheless, Ali used the famous rope-a-dope tactic to perfection and brilliantly defeated Foreman and made history in the process. This was truly a case of mind over matter.

Ali's reliance on the mental as a way of overcoming the physical was quite impressive. This is what Jordan began doing also, using his superior knowledge of the game to defeat younger players, who were closer to their athletic gifts but not as sharp with their mental skills. For all the spectacular dunks and gravity-defying moves that had originally made Jordan famous, it is this postretirement Jordan that I find most interesting.

Take for example the now-famous "flu game" from 1987, when Jordan took control of the finals while visibly battling the flu. As Jordan went to the sideline near the end of the game, his teammate Scottie Pippen had to grab him and hold him up before he completely collapsed to the floor. The point is, Jordan, though physically hampered by both the flu and an aging of his athletic skills, was still superior on the court due to his erudite "basketball IQ."

This notwithstanding, Jordan could not play forever, and the erosion of his physical skills made it clear that at some point in the relatively near future he would need to retire for good. Jordan retired again after the 1998 season and this time sat out until the fall of 2001. Then in 2001 he returned as a member of the Washington Wizards. Jordan had become an owner with a small stake in the Wizards franchise back in 2000. Upon his return, Jordan was at times still a good basketball player, but he was nowhere near the Jordan of old. He was really a shadow of his former self, but for a man of thirty-nine he held his own. It was clear though that he was far from being the best player in the league now.

Between 1998 and 2001 it was already clear that Jordan was gone and that some other players would have to carry the league, even if they probably could never command the same sort of attention that Jordan had garnered. Jordan was such a prominent image in the NBA when he played that it was really unfair to compare other players to him, especially those of a younger generation. There were legions of players who had grown up watching Jordan play, but they grew up at a different time in history than he had.

THE Transition

Jordan had been a child of the immediate post–civil rights era and came of age at a time when Black culture was still primarily ruled by an assimilationist sensibility. In other words, Black youths like Jordan were encouraged to put their best face forward and demonstrate to those in power and to the world at large that Black people knew how to play by the rules and could excel in anything if given the right opportunity. Jordan, he of a Southern Black middle-class upbringing, knew this well and was able to rely on this knowledge when constructing his popular and highly profitable public persona.

Michael Jordan had grown up in an era when affirmative action still provided African Americans with possibilities. Affirmative action never displaced qualified White workers with unqualified Black workers, as the racist perception might suggest. It did, however, offer those who were in a position to take advantage of whatever opportunities might potentially be available a chance to make it into the mainstream, however slim that chance might be. With this sense of possibility fueling the era, Jordan was able to rise to prominence and cash in on that celebrity in a way that no one else before him had. He was a beneficiary of good timing, indeed. The world was ready to accept a Black icon now, and Jordan brilliantly fit the part.

The generation that came after Jordan came from a different time and place. Having grown up in the Reagan '80s, these new ballplayers were not necessarily interested in assimilating. They had grown up in a very hostile racial environment, made that way by Reagan fanning the fires of prejudice. As crack cocaine began to ravage the ghetto in the mid-'80s, many draconian laws were passed, bolstering the growth of the prison industrial complex. The result of this was the massive incarceration of young Black men in increasingly large numbers.

The sense of being that was now informing young Black America had changed quite drastically since the days when Jordan had come of age. In addition, Jordan had demonstrated how successful one could be playing basketball and marketing oneself as a cultural entity in the process. With few other avenues for economic advancement and opportunity open to them, basketball had now become a way of life for many young Black men in the 'hood. This was to be their ticket to a better life, the chance to pull themselves and their whole entourage and extended families up by their Nike Air Force One straps.

Jordan had also, unwittingly, created a cult of the individual in the NBA. He was the star and there was no question about that. Jordan had created very high expectations; however, the times were not conducive to someone like Jordan coming into the game again anytime soon. Jordan was one of a kind, and again, like Ali, a true representative of his era. You don't often see such things twice, and certainly not in succession. This did not stop many of the new players who came on the scene from assuming that they could "be like Mike," that they were unquestioned stars who had come to carry their teams to greatness, but they were sadly mistaken.

Grant Hill, a decent player, proved not to be the upper-middle-class savior that many wanted him to be. Penny Hardaway was even less of a threat to the throne. Shaquille O'Neal was also quite good, but as a literal giant he would have a hard time being accepted as a cultural icon like Jordan had been, because his size was just too enormous for people to see him as anything other than a freak of nature.

The two young players with the most energy and potentially the most promise, though, were on the horizon. Both were drafted in 1996, but few would have suspected that either one of them could carry the torch, and ultimately carry it for completely different reasons. These individuals were Allen Iverson and Kobe Bryant. Both would, over time, develop into great basketball players. Their distinct individual styles would come to be compared to Jordan's, in ways that both affirmed Jordan's dominance and contradicted it also.

THE CHANGING OF THE GUARDS

The NBA has always provided great visual images that assist in creating the theater that basketball has become. One of most significant symbolic images in league history was formed during the 1996–97 season. This image involved Michael Jordan and the young rookie from

Georgetown, Allen Iverson. Though Jordan was the reigning king of basketball at this time, one knew that the time would soon come when he would have to stop playing. In addition, what else could Jordan accomplish? He had won every individual award possible. His team had become the dominant force in the '90s. He had simply vanquished all who stood in his way. It often seemed as though Jordan were playing against himself, as all competitors seemed to wither in his presence.

I often compare Jordan's ascent to that represented in Bruce Lee's *Game of Death* (1978). In the film, which Lee was shooting when he died, the master goes in a house, and on each ascending floor there is a different style of martial arts he must contend with. Lee defeats all his challengers in succession, including Kareem Abdul-Jabbar, who was on the top floor. Jabbar had actually been a student of Bruce Lee's in real life. Jordan performed a similar feat, defeating all his challengers in ascending order; Isiah and the Pistons, Magic Johnson and the Lakers, Clyde Drexler, his boy Charles Barkley, and Karl Malone of the Utah Jazz. Along the way his Bulls team established the best regular-season record of all time.

There was one player, though, who Jordan did not dispense of so easily. This was the man who called himself "The Answer," an appropriate designation if ever there was one. Was Iverson "the answer" to Jordan? That was the question.

Iverson, like all of his contemporaries, had grown up at a time when Michael Jordan was the undisputed king of basketball. While a star at Georgetown, Iverson even wore the exclusive Air Jordan 11 shoes. Air Jordans, or "Jordans" as they are often called, were without a doubt the shoes that separated the platinum from the white gold. Each year a new style of the shoe was released to the public, each with a number that distinguished it from all others. All of the shoes are cult favorites, but the "11s" have always been special. Jordan had a hand in designing all of the shoes. On this pair, he choose to add a touch of class by outlining the shoe in black patent leather against white nylon. This chiaroscuro look was very much like the old "spectators" that real playas and jazz musicians wore back in the day. Jordan said he wanted to add some "formality" to the game. In addition, Jordan wore the 11s during that famous record-breaking 72–10 1995–96 season. By wearing these Jordans, Iverson suggested that he was indeed honoring Michael's attendant greatness. Some also said that he was trying to "be like Mike."

Iverson was not Jordan, nor was he trying to be. He may have admired Jordan's level of excellence and desired the same for himself, but he was not interested in embracing Jordan as his role model. For as much as Iverson saw Jordan as great, he probably also saw him as very much an establishment figure. Jordan had become an acceptable Black media icon who transcended cultural barriers around the globe. In order for him to be so widely embraced, he had to offer an image that was potentially appealing to multiple parties simultaneously.

Iverson was not at all concerned about appealing to multiple interests. Instead, as rapper Tupac Shakur once suggested, Iverson's style was "strictly for my niggas." The Answer was notably influenced by hip hop culture and made no attempt at all to hide it. He stepped on the NBA court with his hair braided in "cornrows," an African American style that was popular back in the '70s. Cornrows are a braided style that had originally been worn by guys while they were in the penitentiary. These long braids were very precise and done close to the scalp. Though they were a staple of those in the pen, they quickly became quite popular in ghetto communities throughout the country. I vividly remember as a child seeing cats sit on the porch, perched between the legs of some girl or woman who was braiding their hair. At the time, though, cornrows tended to be worn at home or in the neighborhood but not in school or at work.

By the '90s, though, cornrows had come back in vogue, like most things retro have come back because of hip hop. Snoop Doggy Dogg shocked everyone when he began wearing cornrows on a regular basis in the early '90s. This provided the connection between gangsta rap and the penitentiary, which figured prominently into this overall narrative. D'Angelo, the neo-soul pioneer, had donned his braids on the cover of his instant classic album *Brown Sugar* in 1995 and added even more cachet to the controversial style.

Cornrows are without a doubt a ghetto hairstyle, emphasizing the lower-class sensibility of the self-proclaimed thugs in the 'hood who wear them. They signal an allegiance to thug life personified. In an NBA where people were still fuming about the new length of the shorts, cornrows were out of the question. Yet when Iverson, Latrell Sprewell, and Rasheed Wallace, among others, started sporting them, the NBA had a major new and potentially more serious style war issue, rooted in both race and class. Iverson's cornrows would soon be as influential as Jordan's bald dome had been some years before.

AI also sported tattoos all over his body, and this too could be said to emerge from the cult of penitentiary chic. Soon tattoos started to appear across the bodies of a number of the league's players. With Iverson the combination of cornrows and tattoos made for a particularly interesting visual statement when he hit the floor. The league was so concerned about containing Iverson's image when he appeared on the cover of an NBA promotional magazine, editors decided to airbrush away his tattoos so as to present what they considered a more acceptable representation of the player.

Unlike the clean-shaven head that Jordan and many others had sported, or the "clean" sartorial style that they donned off the court, Iverson forwarded a very different aesthetic. He and his followers were far from "clean." They were hip hop, and hip hop is potentially "flossy" but never clean. Real hip hop is grimy, and AI was a walking, dribbling embodiment of this sensibility.

Many in the hip hop generation have rejected the formality of suits and ties. Wearing such attire is seen as indicative of not being "real." In their minds the question is, why should people change anything about themselves to accommodate someone or something else? Instead, hip hop fashion is about being comfortable and unrestrained. Being consistent and committed to one's values is cherished in this world. Contrary to what many would say, hip hop has a sense of style, a strong sense of style even; it is simply not style in the traditional sense.

There is a great story about former New Jersey Nets coach Butch Beard demanding that Derrick Coleman wear a suit and tie on road trips. Coleman refused, and Beard said he would fine him until he did. Coleman is said to have given Beard a blank check. The point here is that Coleman was so committed to the hip hop style that he was willing to pay excessive fines for the freedom to maintain that style. As modern NBA players like Coleman see it, their big salaries enable them to buy the right to exercise the freedom to express their individual style.

This attitude does not go over well with the league establishment. Iverson was branded an outlaw for his allegiance to hip hop style and its attendant politics. His style though was only part of the image problem that he posed for the league's and the culture's gatekeepers. Iverson, who had a great first season capped off by winning the Rookie of the Year award, was soon designated NBA public enemy number one.

At one point during his inaugural season, Iverson's squad went up against Jordan and the Bulls, and the resulting fallout in terms of the perceptions of young and old was fascinating. Iverson had come to be known for his impressive "crossover" dribble, one of the hottest moves in basketball. Joe Dumars had set it off originally when the Pistons were in the midst of their title runs in the late '80s/early '90s. Shortly thereafter, Tim Hardaway would become famous for this move while playing at Golden State. Many often called Hardaway's signature crossover the "Texas two-step," referencing his days as a collegian at the University of Texas at El Paso. But Iverson added his own artistic spin to the whole thing when he arrived in the league.

To execute the move, the ball handler quickly switches hands or "crosses over" his dribble so as to catch the defender off balance. When it is done properly, the ball handler will lull the defender to sleep by switching hands repeatedly and appearing to move in one direction, then quickly switching to the other side before finally, and suddenly, picking up the dribble and driving to the basket with lightning speed. The defender is left standing in his tracks, having been momentarily frozen, hypnotized even, by the repeated dribbling. It is an impressive move and one that leaves the defender embarrassed for having been deceived and "clowned" by such sleight of hand.

Iverson's crossover was so effective that the league had to contemplate changing the rules about carrying the basketball, because many claimed that Iverson carried the ball over when he began his move. The fact is that Iverson was so good that observers assumed he could not do such a thing without carrying the ball. No one could believe that he was able to move so fast.

During this regular season game between Philadelphia and Chicago, Iverson found himself being guarded by Jordan. Jordan had been a great defender early in his career. He was starting to show his age somewhat on the defensive end as time passed, however. Jordan especially had trouble guarding shorter, quicker guards. And without question Iverson was the quickest in the league. When Iverson saw this mismatch, he began salivating. The crossover move he put on Jordan was so impressive and at the same time unbelievable because Jordan was not someone people were accustomed to seeing embarrassed in that way.

This was the first time that Jordan actually appeared to be human on a basketball court. It exposed his vulnerability to this new-style maneuver performed by this new-style player. Furthermore, it signaled that there were now younger players in the league who had better physical gifts than Jordan. Most stunning of all, it was the first indication that Jordan's reign was about to come to an end. The Orlando Magic and Nick Anderson had exposed Jordan somewhat in the '95 playoffs. That was immediately after Jordan had returned to basketball. He clearly was not in basketball shape. Jordan ultimately avenged this momentary aberration with a four-game sweep of Anderson and Orlando in the playoffs the following year. All these momentary doubts were forgotten, though, until AI rocked Jordan's world.

During this same game against Iverson, there were also words exchanged between the two players. Jordan is reported to have scolded Iverson, telling him that he had to respect him and what the Bulls had accomplished. Iverson is said to have responded that he does not respect anyone on the court. This became a big deal in the media and the general public.

When the story made the rounds, it was assumed that Iverson meant that he did not respect anyone, period. This comment was used, along with the cornrows and tattoos, to paint Iverson as the new NBA villain. He was castigated for his style and now his words. Iverson had become emblematic, for many people, of what was wrong with the NBA. He was now the poster child for the new generation of hip hop ballers, and, believe me, this was not meant as a compliment.

In the eyes of his critics, Iverson was a young man from an impoverished background who had been fortunate enough to make large sums of money playing in the NBA. They wanted him to be grateful. From AI's point of view, he saw this as an opportunity that he had earned by virtue of his skill, and he felt no need to be humble. As he saw it, humility was not even in the equation and Iverson was far from humble. He was not just confident in his ability, he was also fearless. The danger he had encountered growing up was such that any rhetorical danger he might get into with the league establishment and the public at large seemed nonexistent to him. He had money, and this money was a result of his incredible playing skills. Iverson thus did not have to care about anything else. He did not respect tradition, or, more accurately, he did not buy into the tradition. He was not grateful to be there. Nor was he really concerned about what others might have to say about his attitude or actions. In other words, in true hip hop fashion, he did not give a fuck!

If there are two things that indicate the cultural politics of hip hop most, they are the idea of "keepin' it real," which is about honesty, and "not giving a fuck," which is also about honoring one's convictions whatever they may be, regardless of the circumstances. Iverson personified both of these ideological edicts, and for this he became an NBA outcast almost immediately.

AI often traveled with his "boys," a group of friends, many of whom go back to his days growing up in the 'hoods of Hampton, Virginia. These friends were so visibly connected to the "thug life" mentality and way of life that they put fear in the minds of many who saw them and their close relationship to Iverson. The media often referred to these guys as AI's posse, and this impression was also connected to the presence of hip hop in the culture. The media and mainstream White society often imply that large groups of Black men constitute a gang, and this was also what was said about Iverson. White guys have friends; Black guys have a posse. This tends to be the thinking.

Of course, Iverson did nothing to dissuade anyone from thinking this, either, except to proclaim that these were his friends and he was going to stick by them. Many of the hip hop generation see their "people" as instrumental to their existence. For them, it is an expression of loyalty and of a need to stay connected to their roots. As they see it, why should one change and get a group of new friends simply because one is now making money? In observance of this code of conduct, Iverson refused to change with the wind. He stuck to his guns, no pun intended, and stuck with his homeys.

So Allen Iverson was not a well-liked figure among the league brass, the predominantly older White media, and the middle-American White fans, nor among many conservative Black fans, either. Ironically, one of Iverson's most vocal critics was Charles Barkley. The man who once said he was "not a role model" felt that Iverson was selfish and presented a troubling image. Yet Iverson was a big hit with young people all over the country who made his #3 Philadelphia 76ers jersey the best-selling jersey in the NBA. He had become the king of hip hop ball, and his refusal to change his style, attitude, and overall disposition endeared him to many people weaned on the influence of hip hop itself.

As word began to spread that Iverson often was late to or just straight out missed practice altogether, this added to the animosity that many felt toward him. It also made him seem that much more admirable to his supporters. This open flouting of the rules and blatant disregard for tradition and authority attracted as many lovers as it did haters. AI had become, in the words of Ice Cube, "the nigga you love to hate." He had also become the new face of young, urban Black men everywhere, who saw their dreams played out when they looked at Iverson. They saw his immense success and his equally immense desire to do things his way and suffer the consequences accordingly. He was real, no doubt!

Just before the 2000–2001 season began, it was reported that Iverson was releasing a hip hop record. He was not the first pro basketball player to do this. Shaquille O'Neal had dabbled poorly in rap for a few years, starting in the early '90s. After originally appearing on the *Arsenio Hall Show* rapping with the group Fu Schnickens, Shaq launched his own hip hop career. Over time Shaq sold a lot of records but was never taken seriously as a rap artist. There was even an album released in the mid-'90s called *B Ball's Best Kept Secrets*, which featured a plethora of basketball players trying to demonstrate their hip hop skills. This too was a joke. Yet, because Iverson's album was rooted in the hard-core gangsta rap tradition, the anticipation of his album created a firestorm before it was ever released. People began circling the wagons early on and criticized the album repeatedly for its incendiary language. Iverson eventually decided, or perhaps it was decided for him, not to release the record.

The Philadelphia 76ers had an incredible season in 2000–2001, making it all the way to the NBA finals. Iverson was voted the league's most valuable player for his outstanding efforts. He had led the 76ers virtually by himself, à la early Jordan, taking a group of role players on his back in pursuit of a championship. As the finals approached, many of the same people who had been so critical of him now openly celebrated his effort and desire. Because Iverson was so little, in what was clearly a big man's game, his success was that much more impressive. Had Iverson changed? Had he started to listen to his coach, Larry Brown, a figure with whom he had clashed often? Had he mellowed with old age? Had he seen the error of his ways?

The answer to all these questions was a resounding no! Iverson was the same player, the same person he had always been. It's just that now he was winning, and America loves a winner. When the nation got a chance to see his unrelenting attitude on the court as his team advanced through the playoffs, they saw how this undersized man with the big heart came to play every night. When Iverson played through numerous injuries in the process, they saw a real fighter and a real winner. And in spite of what had been reported about him previously, people could see for themselves that Iverson was indeed "The Answer," in no uncertain terms.

Things seemed to revert back to old form though when Iverson was injured a great deal of the 2001–2002 season, and his team exited the playoffs in the first round. Iverson was again harshly criticized in public by Larry Brown for missing practice and other transgressions. He was even reported to have been the subject of trade rumors because of his continued refusal to act in the way that Brown and the team wanted him to. The news media also climbed back on the anti-Iverson bandwagon, castigating him all over again for the same things they had been critical of in the past. Iverson was once again the problem child, proving that winning always hides a multitude of sins.

When Iverson was winning he was considered a changed man. But when he was injured and his team lost, he was said to be derelict in his duties. Iverson, though, remained true to his character and blew off his critics during a humorous, though clearly acrimonious, press conference after the conclusion of the season. He was visibly and audibly miffed that people would continue to question his desire after he had repeatedly demonstrated how committed he was on the court. The issue of not going to practice every day, for example, is one that is constantly used to needle him. Yet Iverson is of the mind-set that even though he does not practice, his game has remained strong doing things the way he has always done them. In hip hop parlance, Iverson could be said to be "doin' me," and that's all about being true to oneself.

The point here is that Iverson represents a square peg, and the establishment is trying to force him into this round hole of conformity. The media, the league, and many fans are of a different generation, and certainly of a different orientation than that of hip hop. Iverson embodies this notion of "ashy to classy" that Biggie Smalls once referenced, and this has to do with achieving success on his own terms and having the money and cultural capital to define one's own existence. Iverson, then, is a living example of the hip hop sentiment expressed by Jay-Z, who said "we didn't cross over, we bought the suburbs to the 'hood."

Fans of the game, Black, White, and otherwise, who have knowledge of hip hop and its cultural politics, see Iverson in a completely different way than those "haters" who seek to stagnate his process. The hip hop generation sees Iverson as real, as authentic, and as someone who achieved success by doing things his way, and who refuses to change just because someone else says he should. Iverson too seems to have recognized his own evolution. He wore Dr. J's number 6 in the 2002 All-Star Game, which was played in Philadelphia. It was a conscious expression of his respect for J's game and understanding of the need to embrace history as opposed to being so openly dismissive of it.

Ultimately the cult of love and hate that surrounds AI is consistent with the way society often treats its celebrities. There is always a thin line between love and hate when situations like this are at work. Everyone loves a villain, be it Jesse James, Tony Soprano, or Allen Iverson. Of course, many also hate those who attempt to do things their own way, especially when these iconoclasts are young Black men who come from a completely different world and worldview than those who are in power.

In my mind, Allen Iverson and what he represents are among the most interesting developments to come about in the NBA in quite some time. Iverson is indicative of the influence of hip hop on basketball, and on American culture in general. And like hip hop, he uses his own distinct style to attract legions of people to watch him perform. Iverson is a basketball player and a conscious social statement all in one. His money and his fame make him hard to ignore, and his politics of style have made him a cultural icon. Only time will tell how this all evolves and how we will regard The Answer when he can no longer cross people over. Will he remain controversial? Or will he, like one of his most vocal critics, Charles Barkley, mellow with age? Who knows? But the ride promises to be one where there is never a dull moment.

Karaoke

During that same 1996 draft in which Iverson was selected by Philadelphia with the first pick, the Charlotte Hornets selected a high school prodigy from the suburbs of the City of Brotherly Love. The talented high school 'baller, Kobe Bryant, was immediately traded to the Los Angeles Lakers for Lakers starting center Vlade Divac. Who was this guy?

Players like Darryl Dawkins, aka "Chocolate Thunder," had made the move straight from high school and lasted for some years in the NBA. But none were as successful as Moses Malone had been when he came into the game in the '70s, at least not over the long haul. Kevin Garnett had come straight from high school the year before Bryant, and his first year had been decent enough. This was all Bryant needed. Now here he was, Kobe Bryant, son of former 76er guard Joe "Jellybean" Bryant, attempting to play in the NBA as a small forward or two guard, lacking the height advantage that had in times past helped compensate for the inexperience of players who were trying to go pro right after high school. Many felt that Bryant was destined to fail.

When people use the word "prodigy," they refer to individuals who excel in the world of high art and culture; a child pianist, for instance. Kobe Bryant, though, is very much a prodigy. He is also an interesting contrast to Iverson, as his class status defies the perceived ghetto stereotype of most NBA players. Kobe is an upper-middle-class Black guy who grew up between Italy and the suburbs. He is not from the 'hood, and his actions seem to indicate that he probably has never been there either, not even on a tour.

The class contrast between Iverson and Bryant is quite interesting in that it reveals the line of demarcation that informs many thoughts about the NBA now, particularly since the league is overwhelmingly Black. In other words, Blackness, as I have said elsewhere, is the norm in the NBA. Therefore, class becomes a more significant concept in analyzing the cultural representation that the league foregrounds. This being the case, Kobe Bryant has often functioned as the league's de facto White man, in that his upper-middle-class status is more easily assimilated into the game's overall fabric than the hip hop–inspired narrative that Allen Iverson embodies.

Kobe Bryant began playing basketball when he was a child in Milan and while his father was dominating the Italian professional league as a player. This experience allowed him to learn to speak Italian and also gave him a unique point of view when he returned to live in the United States as a teenager. Kobe scored extremely high on his SAT and could have attended any college in the nation. He was not some ghetto dweller from a poor public high school who had been more athlete than student. He was smart and athletically gifted. He was the perfect combination of talent and intellect, recalling Grant Hill, who was Black, educated, and upper-middle-class, as well as a fierce basketball player. Kobe Bryant would have been tailor-made for Duke basketball with this pedigree. Instead, he chose to go pro. This confounded many, however, because he was clearly not doing it to support his family financially, as is the usual claim made by "hardship" athletes. Bryant just wanted to test his immense skills at the pro level. It was a want, not a need.

Bryant entered the league still a teenager, and though it was almost a foregone conclusion that he was going to need time to develop, he jumped right into the mix and immediately demonstrated incredible skills for someone so young. Bryant was not shy or conservative. He tended to shoot the ball every time he got it. It often seemed as though he was playing by himself.

Kobe was, as he had been back in Italy, off in his own world. He was too young to fully participate in the NBA's social life and too suburban to roll with the urban ethos that had come to consume the league itself. The young basketball player was not what you would necessarily call hip hop, either. His style, his manner, and his overall disposition was unique to who he was, and there was certainly no one else like Kobe playing NBA basketball.

Unlike Iverson, Kobe was not the seemingly nihilistic, hard-edged, urban nightmare who dismissed the importance of previous generations and had contempt for authority. No, Kobe was, in keeping with his class background, simply a spoiled brat. Whereas Iverson was roundly criticized for missing practice, Kobe was at practice before anyone else and still there when everyone else was gone. The media proved to be a nemesis for Allen Iverson, while Kobe seemed to enjoy nothing more than doing interviews. Iverson crossed over Jordan, as it were, with blatant disrespect, and embarrassed the man in the process, while staking his own claim to future greatness. Kobe, on the other hand, though certainly interested in eclipsing Jordan, as evidenced by his attempts to take it to Jordan in the 1998 All-Star Game, was very much into being like Mike. Kobe's infatuation with Jordan clearly demonstrated that imitation was the sincerest form of flattery. And while Allen Iverson had an aborted hip hop record, Kobe dabbled in an R&B project that was never released either.

In other words, the two could not be more opposite. The only thing they remotely have in common is being drafted the same year and the Philadelphia connection. Even the Philly connection was specious though, because the fans in the city loudly booed their departed home-town hero Kobe Bryant during the 2002 All-Star Game.

Allen Iverson and Kobe Bryant faced off in the 2000–2001 NBA finals, and though the Lakers dominated the series, the differences between the two players were something that could finally be seen up close. It was compelling to watch this unfold on the floor. At the conclusion of game two, in LA, with the Lakers about to even the series, Bryant began yapping in Iverson's direction. It is Iverson who has a reputation for talking shit, for being street. But here was Kobe doing all the talking.

Iverson seemed surprised at first. He began exhorting his team-mates, clapping his hands, but Kobe interrupted him. Kobe said that he knew Iverson was trying to motivate his team, but "I don't care." He went on to tell him that the road to the championship runs through LA. Kobe repeated his comments to Iverson in the postgame press conference. Iverson meanwhile would not divulge the contents of their exchange when quizzed by reporters. What was interesting about this was seeing the stunned look on Iverson's face as he witnessed this streetlike atti-tude coming from the normally aloof Kobe Bryant. It was like the sub-urban kid had decided to talk shit to the embodiment of thug life personified—a completely stunning role reversal, indeed. This was out of character, it seemed, but it was also quite telling.

Kobe Bryant was not like his fellow NBA brethren. He had not grown up in the ghetto. He was not his family's financial savior. The game was his passion, but not a life-or-death matter to him in the way that it was to so many others. Kobe was someone who had a unique upbringing. By virtue of these circumstances he had learned to play the game of bas-ketball very much in solitude. And like a true virtuoso, he used these solitary moments to refine his game. In this regard, Kobe is indicative of someone who has perfected his craft in the age of virtual reality. He is very much a product of the digital age.

As the story goes, Kobe, while living in Italy, would wait for the postman to deliver care packages from family members back home in the States. Yet he was not as interested in receiving home-cooked deli-cacies as he was in watching the videotapes of NBA games that they sent over. This was his master's course, and he studied Jordan and Magic, among others, with the passion of a determined graduate student. He was especially interested in Jordan, as one might expect, even to the point of repeatedly watching and absorbing Jordan's demeanor during his media interviews. In the stages of his pro career, Kobe often sounded just like Jordan when doing interviews, right down to the cadence of his voice. Kobe was so influenced by Jordan that he would often scowl in the exact manner that Jordan did. There was something uniquely postmodern about all of this; simulation at the highest level.

With Michael Jordan being such a visible media icon, Kobe had an ample supply of imagery from which to choose. When the Lakers won their first championship in 2000, Kobe's cradling and kissing of the championship trophy was a complete reenactment of Jordan doing the same some years earlier. It was as though Jordan had been cloned. Michael Jordan as Kobe Bryant, Kobe Bryant as Michael Jordan. Where did one start and the other end? It was quite hard to tell. Kobe was not simply interested in being the next Jordan, he was interested in being Jordan!

His aloof, privileged disposition made Kobe seem like a spoiled rich kid, a distinct contrast to the brooding, angry malcontent, which was the image that most of the league's other stars carried around when things were not right with them. One need only look back to the press conference Kobe held to announce his intention to enter into the NBA in 1996. With his sunglasses perched ever-so-cool on top of his head, he declared that he was ready to test his game in the NBA. The arrogance and confidence of this image set the tone and foreshadowed what was to come once he became a star in the league.

The funny thing was that Kobe seemed to have a great affinity with the kids. However, he was not a big fan favorite among adults, nor was he particularly popular with the other players in the league, including some of his own teammates. When rumors began circulating that Kobe and teammate Shaquille O'Neal were mired in the midst of a divisive and potentially destructive feud during the 2000–2001 season, the young star appeared to be on the wrong side of popular opinion. Whether the beef was fueled by who got more commercials or who took the most shots, it was a telling episode in the life of the young, Black, rich and famous.

Clearly the reason that the Lakers were so dominant had to do with the maturation of Shaq, the game's most dominant big man in many years. Unlike in previous times in the league, Shaq had no peer at center. Fewer and fewer traditional big men were even in the league, and none of them were equipped to deal with Shaq. Blessed with size, power, and awesome skill, Shaq was unstoppable. His horrible free throw shooting notwithstanding, Shaq was by far the best player in the NBA, and his dominance was such that it made for a lack of competition. As long as Shaq was on his game, forget about it. He could not be stopped. This opened up Kobe's game. With Shaq being such a force inside, Kobe had a lot of freedom to play his wide open style and create even more troubling mismatches for opponents.

But instead of accepting this, Kobe went about pursuing his own greatness. He would not meet Shaq halfway. Kobe was not only pursuing championships, he was also pursuing greatness and striving to define his own legacy in the game—all of this well before his twenty-fifth birthday. It was seen as selfish. Kobe's arrogant disposition made the perception that much more viable. Kobe was not known for hanging out with his teammates. He barely spoke to them off the court. Kobe is reported as saying that Dennis Rodman was the perfect teammate, because the two of them had never spoken off the court.

Whereas someone like Iverson was threatening to the status quo, Kobe was not, but he was roundly disliked. The booing at the 2002 All-Star Game was indicative of this. Kobe joked about not needing any tickets for any friends during the NBA finals in Philly in 2001 because they were all 76er fans. He had grown up in Philly, but he had no connection to his hometown whatsoever. Philly fans are known for their hostility, often toward their own team, so this was no surprise. Kobe's reaction to it was.

When asked after the game how he felt getting booed in his own hometown, he admitted that it hurt and seemed to be on the verge of tears. This open display of emotion was quite different from the "I don't give a fuck" attitude that most NBA players typically display. Kobe sounded like a wounded pup as opposed to a vicious rottweiler. This was not in keeping with the hip hop aesthetic of showing no emotion and acting as though a diss was really a blessing in disguise. Kobe appeared vulnerable, and maybe for the first time in his NBA career he seemed to be human. He was such a construction beforehand, that this moment made him appear more "real" and less an egregious personality.

There have been other signs that Kobe is still a work in progress. At the end of Kobe's rookie season back in 1997, the self-assured youngster had the ball in his hands at the end of a close playoff game against the Utah Jazz. Kobe, only a year removed from playing high school games, was now caught up in the ebb and flow of an NBA playoff contest. With the game hanging in the balance, Kobe shot four air balls between the end of regulation and overtime. The Lakers lost the game, and Kobe's continued failure to even hit the rim was pretty embarrassing. If ever there was a moment when he looked to be in over his head in this grown man's league, this was it. The humiliation of shooting four air balls, four shots that didn't even touch the basket and drew nothing but air, was the height of public embarrassment, especially for an ambitious kid like Kobe. This moment was an all-time low, yet it demonstrated that Kobe was not scared to be the goat and that he was not afraid to be a failure. This was quite telling. It was again an indication of good things to come, if you were looking for the silver lining inside the cloud that had become Kobe's world.

By the 2002 conference finals, Kobe had moved far away from the humiliation of those four air balls in Utah. He had won two championships with the Lakers and, though struggling mightily in the trenches trying to beat the Sacramento Kings, Kobe was on the verge of winning a third straight championship. When the highly entertaining and competitive series finally concluded, Kobe ran up to the Kings' Mike Bibby and embraced him. Bibby had made a name for himself with outstanding play that kept Sacramento in the series. During the embrace, Kobe began telling Bibby, in the best street slang, what an amazing job he had done and how much he respected him as a player. The scene was quite compelling and recalled the moment between Isiah Thomas and Kevin

McHale back in 1988 when the Pistons defeated the Celtics. McHale told Isiah that when he and the Pistons went out to LA to face the Lakers, that he should not be happy just making it to the finals for the first time, but that they should go out there to win.

Kobe had seemingly grown as a player. More important, he had matured as a man. This was wonderful to see. At one time Kobe didn't even look to pass the ball to his teammates. Now, no longer the loner out to change the game all by himself, he was even complimenting his opponents.

By the 2002 finals, Kobe was wearing "throwback" jerseys to the arena. He carefully chose an array of jerseys from past champions of several different sports: Jackie Robinson, Wayne Gretzky, and Joe Montana. In what turned out to be a most surreal instance, evoking the best of David Lynch, Kobe strolled into the last game of the finals wearing, what else, none other than Michael Jordan's famous #23 Bulls jersey.

In early July 2003, Kobe Bryant was charged with the sexual assault of a nineteen-year-old woman in Eagle County, Colorado. Many initially reacted with surprise and shock, because, as I've stated earlier, Bryant is considered above the fray. The media has portrayed him as a nice, inoffensive, upper-middle-class Black man who just happens to be surrounded by a bunch of other "thug ass niggas." Some people have even speculated that Bryant's brush with the law will bring him instant "street cred," something he has been accused of lacking in the past, but I doubt it. Street credibility is about being authentic and has nothing to do with being charged as a criminal. If anything, Kobe defied every imaginable code of Black masculinity at his press conference after the charges were announced. Stitting on stage, holding his wife's hand, admitting to adultery, though denying any criminal deeds, he sobbed and begged like a baby, and in so doing further distanced himself from the streets. As a matter of fact, the streets would characterize Kobe's actions as that of a "lil bitch." Bryant's performance may prove smart down the line during the actual trial, but it might guarantee that he'll never be fully embraced by the streets. A court of law is one thing, but something tells me that in this case the court of the streets will hand down the final verdict.

Can It Be All So Simple?
Internationally Known, Nationally Recognized, and Locally Accepted

ne quick glance at the world of basketball today, and it is immediately obvious that the game is very different than it was back in 1979. This was the year that the Magic/Bird rivalry set in motion the forces that would create a modern-day league with an urban style and a global audience. A confluence of television, marketable stars, compelling social narratives, and changes in the cultural landscape of America has been instrumental in helping to make basketball the sport that most defines this present moment of our social and cultural history.

Over this period of time basketball has brought urban culture front and center, and has highlighted a number of potentially volatile issues. The game then is a useful surrogate for engaging larger themes of race, class, and identity. Despite the league's recognition of this new world order and the presence of an emergent and affluent Black ruling class in the sport, the old-world specter of racism still lingers in the rafters of NBA arenas. It shows up in public attitudes about playing style, appearance, and salaries, among other issues. The profound influence of hip hop culture on the new generation of NBA players—these young, Black, rich and famous men—only complicates the dynamics at work. This sit-

uation makes the NBA both important and interesting as a kind of social laboratory. Basketball is now a stage where the drama of these social
concerns gets played out on a regular basis. Though often entertaining,
it is far from being just a game, it is a lesson in life and a compelling narrative for understanding the social and cultural machinations of the
twenty-first century.

When Magic and Bird started waging war back in the late '70s, the
league was a perfect mirror of America, or so it seemed. The game was
somewhat equally divided between Black and White, though leaning in
the direction of Black, and it tended to play out along these lines. The
Black/White dynamic was on display as evidenced by the Lakers/Celtics
rivalry, for instance. Now, with the majority of the players in the NBA being Black, and with the predominant style of the league being what it is,
one finds these old distinctions do not hold up nearly as well. At the
same time, America is no longer simply a Black/White affair. Though
this contrast will forever inform life in this country, as it is at the foundation of America's history, it is no longer the singular expression of cultural identity that it once was. America is now a place where a diverse
group of people defines the population. And in a digital world without
borders, the entire cultural landscape has changed drastically.

In other words, the Black/White contrast is no longer the exclusive
way of understanding what is really going on in the world around us.
Those who refuse to acknowledge this, those with their heads firmly
planted in the sand, will be as outdated as an old typewriter in a world of
high-speed Internet connections. The game of basketball has certainly
seen the future and has followed suit accordingly. As a matter of fact,
the NBA is, to my mind, at the forefront of recognizing this cultural shift
and incorporating it into its worldview.

Yao Ming, a seven-foot-five center from the People's Republic of
China, had NBA general managers and coaches salivating when he announced that he would be available for the 2002 draft. Ming held private workouts before the draft to demonstrate his skills for fawning team
executives. Ming was eventually selected by the Houston Rockets as the
first pick in the 2002 draft. This lofty draft position was once reserved

for the American college player with the most potential. Now that is clearly a thing of the past.

Ming is obviously tall, but he also possesses the abilities of a guard, having a deft shooting touch and the ability to put the ball on the floor like a much smaller player. Considering that Shaquille O'Neal has seemingly made extinct all other big men during his reign as the game's dominant—and some would argue only real—center, it makes sense that someone like Ming would attract so much attention.

Yao Ming is also representative of the changing face of global politics and its impact. He had to be cleared by the Chinese authorities before he could play in America, and Ming is also responsible for paying a sizable amount of his NBA earnings to the Chinese government as a way of compensating them for what they consider lost services. In the old days of the Cold War, there were always stories of foreign nationals and athletes who hailed from Communist and Eastern Bloc countries defecting to the US in order to play sports. Well now, in this global economy, where China stands as one of the lone Communists in a post–Cold War world, Ming is simply an object of exchange, a commodity, and a way for China to maintain its Communist face while continuing to play its state capitalist hand.

Yao Ming will not be the first Chinese national in the NBA, either. Though his selection as the first pick in the draft is especially noteworthy, he will join former Chinese national teammates Wang Zhizhi, now playing for the Los Angeles Clippers, and Mengke Bateer of the San Antonio Spurs. The three were once dubbed the "Great Walking Wall of China" when they played on the national team. The arrangement has enormous upside potential for the NBA going forward. With over a billion people in China, the future worldwide impact of the NBA is quite promising when you consider the massive television audience inherent in this equation.

I mention Ming and the other Chinese players because they represent the new image of the NBA in this global marketplace. The NBA is no longer a Black/White league like it was in the past. The number of White American professional athletes has consistently declined in numbers over the years, and this is especially true in the NBA. The NBA that Jerry West, Rick Barry, Bill Walton, and Larry Bird played in is long gone. White American athletes are now so scarce that a marginal player like Jason Williams, now of the Memphis Grizzlies, was able to garner a great deal of undeserved attention when he entered the league with the Sacramento Kings back in 1999. Williams was dubbed "White Choco-late" when he came into the league because he supposedly possessed the urban style more often associated with Black players. Many even dared compare Williams to the great "Pistol" Pete Maravich, a White ballplayer and one of the game's true stylists from the '70s. Williams, though, was too young to really have absorbed any of Maravich's signa-ture moves, as he was clearly influenced by Black players like Isiah Thomas or even Allen Iverson. Yet the media seems reluctant to suggest that a White player has been influenced by someone Black.

It is also important to point out that Williams' White working-class disposition helped facilitate his being dubbed White Chocolate. This class status, in some ways, racialized him. Williams, after an impressive start, proved to be a somewhat mediocre player. It became apparent that the only reason he was getting any attention was due to his perceived fish-out-of-water status as a rare White American player in a league dom-inated by Black players and, increasingly, players from other countries.

The overwhelming majority of the White players receiving any sort of recognition now all tend to be from places other than the United States. There is a large contingent of players from the former Yugoslavia, notably from Croatia or Serbia. Many of these players grew up in condi-tions similar to those of an urban American ghetto. This in turn pro-duces what I like to call a sense of "wartorn Whiteness" that is quite different than, say, the conditions present in working-class or middle-class White America. Therefore, to identify a Peja Stojakavich or a Vlade Divac as simply White would be very reductive. There are also now play-ers from many other countries as well, with some of the more notable ones being: Dirk Nowitzki from Germany; Hedo Turkgolu from Turkey; Eduardo Najara from Mexico; Pau Gasol from Spain; Tony Parker from France; Nene Hilario from Brazil; and Jake Tskalidas from Greece. Now when you hear that a player is from Georgia, you cannot assume that the player hails from that state in the southeastern United States; he could just as easily be from the former Soviet republic.

Of course, there have long been a number of prominent Black NBA players from the continent of Africa as well, including the great Hakeem Olajuwan from Nigeria and the defensive stalwart Dikembe Mutombo from what is now the Congo Republic. Both Olajuwan and Mutombo though, unlike the new crop of foreign stars, came along in '80s through the American collegiate ranks before excelling in the pros. The same can also be said of a White Canadian player like Steve Nash.

Whatever their route to the NBA, this group of foreign players, be they Black or White, has altered the cultural balance of the league, and in the process, White American players have been the ones relegated to minority status. Therefore the NBA offers a fascinating representation of global culture in the most diverse sense, with African Americans forming the majority and these other nationalities comprising the rest. It is a picture that mirrors the way of the world in the global marketplace that we now exist in.

Considering that the Internet has digitally erased lines of demarcation that had existed previously, the world has become a smaller place, and the confluence of cultures that is now the NBA makes a bold and monumental statement about this newly defined sense of America's identity in this time. The NBA is also astutely aware of the economic ramifications of this. The more nationalities that are represented, the more potential television markets the league has at its disposal around the world.

What I find most ironic about all of this is that African American players are now the ones who represent America in this new global consortium. The idea of Black people as representative of America is one that would not have been conceivable back in the late '70s. Sure, Black American athletes have for quite some time been prominently featured in the Olympics. The Olympics, for most of their history, were supposedly representative of the best amateur athletes in the world. With this sporting event occurring only every four years, this amateur endeavor was not such that Black people really represented America. These Black athletes were being used by America, and at some point they were powerless while being used. While they were allowed to represent America, they could not represent themselves. Once the games were over and they returned to the States, the individuals in question were unable to fully participate as citizens in American society.

Even though a figure like Jesse Owens was used to bolster America's image abroad in the Berlin Olympics of 1936 during this ultranationalistic time leading up to World War II, he was not treated as an American back here at home. Owens was reduced to racing against cars and horses to subsist, and he was even brought up on tax evasion charges by the same country he had so gallantly represented during its time of need.

Muhammad Ali, then known as Cassius Clay, won an Olympic boxing gold medal at the 1960 games in Rome. He soon found out how much that meant when he tried to eat in a segregated restaurant in his native Louisville upon returning. Clay was denied admission to the segregated facility, and this, as the urban legend goes, prompted him to throw his medal into the Ohio River. He now knew it meant nothing at all. Owens, Clay, and others like them were simply pawns in a larger game of American representation, but they were often discarded once they were no longer needed.

For most of their history Black people have had to exist outside of what is known as mainstream America. Yet this is no longer the case. Though racism still constitutes a major component of America's character, Blackness and America's broader sense of cultural identity has evolved into something quite different from what it was in the past. These basketball players are now wealthy and visible along with being integral components in America's biggest global export, popular culture. The players have more leverage, more agency in their own affairs, and they are no longer just being used when it's convenient to make the country look good. These individuals are now necessary because they comprise the core of America's cultural identity on a global scale.

The world drastically changed shape in the post–Cold War era of the 1990s. Along with this profound shift, the digital revolution altered our sense of being during this time. Considering the way our cultural identity has been challenged in the aftermath of September 11, this redefinition of what is truly American and the way that it is represented in basketball, with Blackness at the center, is quite fascinating indeed.

September 11 exposed the fact, for those who had not noticed or actively chose to ignore it, that America is no longer this exclusively "White" country. Though Whiteness is still considered the norm in America, the rapidly shifting population dynamics of the country have forced a reconsideration of what most accurately defines the nation's cultural identity. Because Whiteness alone can no longer claim exclusive domain over this cultural identity, Blackness, a central component in the equation since slavery, has come to assist America in broadening its sense of representation.

One of America's biggest exports now is entertainment and popular culture. With basketball being one of the most successful examples of this exported pop culture, the representation of Blackness becomes an integral part of the process. In this regard then, an all-American icon like Michael Jordan is as visible, if not more so, as any other White American who might lay claim to this distinction.

The game of basketball is American, and it is resolutely Black. Thus the Serbs, Croatians, Turks, Chinese, and individuals from other cultures who attempt to come into the league are coming into a space as uniquely American as one can imagine. That American space also just happens to be as Black as a thousand midnights. The Blackness that defines basketball now is as American as apple pie, or better yet, as American as peach cobbler.

young brothas incorporated

Like the league itself, the NBA draft over the last few years has tended to foreshadow things to come. With Yao Ming headlining the class of 2002, the global implications for the game and the attendant issues of cultural identity are front and center. The 2001 draft offered another example of the way the game is changing and how this change reflects larger concerns. The Washington Wizards used their first pick in the 2001 draft to select Kwame Brown, a high school player out of Atlanta.

Brown was followed by Tyson Chandler, a high school star straight outta Compton, California. With the fourth pick the Chicago Bulls selected another high school star, Eddie Curry. This meant that three of the first four picks in the 2001 draft were high school players. The trend of drafting young players has gotten to be so popular now that LeBron James, the latest addition to the young, Black, rich and famous, was already being predicted to be the first pick in the 2003 draft when he was still a junior in high school.

Though many high schoolers have excelled in the league, none of them had ever been the very first pick in the draft until Brown was picked in 2001. Kwame Brown and the subsequent selection of the other high school players was the culmination of a trend that had been on the upswing for quite some time.

When the Minnesota Timberwolves selected Kevin Garnett with the fifth overall pick in 1995, it was the highest draft position a high school player had received up to that point. Garnett has become one of the game's best all-around players since that time. Kobe Bryant has said that Garnett's success helped confirm his decision to turn pro straight out of high school in '96. In addition to KG and Kobe, several other players have skipped college, and now it is expected that the best players will routinely jump from prep ball to pro ball.

Tracy McGrady, a high schooler selected in 1997, is one of the best offensive players in the league now. Jermaine O'Neal from the class of 1996 is quickly becoming one of the game's better big men. Darius Miles of the Clippers, the third pick in 2000, has also made an impressive mark for such a young player.

The ascendancy of the high school player has also altered the college game in the process. College players who stay for a full four years are often thought to be flawed in some way; otherwise, the thinking goes, they would have left college earlier. It also seems as though the gatekeepers of college ball have finally gotten their way. The game of college basketball is such that the schools that consistently win now are schools like Stanford or even Utah, schools with a high number of White players. Duke, the school that is possibly the most dominant of big-time college programs, continues to feature its share of middle-class Black players like Shane Battier and Jay Williams, along with White players like Mike Dunleavy. Yet most of the other teams, like Stanford, can now compete because of the parity brought on by the best talent going directly into the pro game. Those supertalented players who do not go directly from high school tend to spend as little time as possible in college. In the past the best players might have left college after three seasons, and a few, like Magic or Isiah, after two years. Now players are considered ancient if they stay longer than one year in college.

As a result, the pro game has become younger and the college game has become Whiter. The two forms of basketball are about as different as one can imagine. College has been able to reclaim its designation as a showcase for "student-athletes," and the NBA has increasingly faced the wrath of those who think that the league has become too young and too Black, not to mention too rich and too famous.

Now that this trend is in place, there suddenly seems to be a backlash against the young players who immediately command large sums of money the minute they get drafted. There have been racially loaded questions asked about the appropriateness of making millionaires out of people who are barely voting age. David Stern, the league's commissioner, has even suggested that the players union institute a minimum age limit that would restrict players under age twenty from competing. This position is supported by many in the media and in society at large. There has always been consternation about the amount of money that Black athletes make, and this has increased. It is now camouflaged as an age issue. Oftentimes those cries about players being too young are really coded discussions about them being too Black.

Interestingly, no one has lodged similar complaints about sports like tennis or gymnastics, where participants often start competing nationally and internationally at an even earlier age than they do in basketball. Tennis, for example, tends to be more White and middle- to upper-middle-class in its orientation, the amazing Venus and Serena Williams notwithstanding. There is no threat to the status quo if a young middle-class White girl like Jennifer Capriati or upper-middle-class figure like Lindsay Davenport starts to make millions on the tennis court. Young middle-class or upper-middle-class White girls with no college education have for years been dominant and financially successful on the tennis court. Yet there is a sense that it is wrong or poses some threat when a young Black man from the 'hood attempts to do the same on the basketball court.

The possibility of an age limit in the NBA speaks to this directly. If enacted, it would represent an overt attempt to forestall the money-making capabilities of young Black men. Though the WTA, which governs woman's pro tennis, has now instituted the so-called "Capriati rule," the age limit is still set at only fifteen, much younger than the age limit of twenty that the NBA is suggesting. This argument about an age limit in the NBA is often shrouded in discussions of "what's best for the kids" or "what's best for the game." This effort to deny economic opportunity is a direct challenge to financial aspirations of potential NBA stars and an overt attempt to prohibit young Black men from becoming rich and famous.

During the 1998 off-season, the NBA and the players union engaged in a very public battle over a new collective bargaining agreement that would govern player contracts and league finances. Consensus would suggest that the NBA won that battle decisively. More important, the league was able to cast the players association as the bad guy in the negotiations by making it appear as though the players were "on strike" as opposed to being "locked out" by the owners, which was the case. By locking out the players, the NBA had in effect forced a work stoppage that resulted in a long portion of the season being canceled until the two sides reached an agreement. The players association, in a largely futile attempt to counter perceptions, took out ads in many major publications declaring that they had been locked out as opposed to being on strike.

There is a big difference between the two positions. To be locked out means that the league does not allow the players to make a living while they are negotiating. To be on strike means that the players themselves decide to stop work. Amid the antiunion atmosphere that has flourished in this country since Ronald Reagan fired all those striking air traffic controllers back in the '80s, this sentiment, coupled with the resentment many feel toward wealthy Black athletes anyway, was quite a lethal combination. The players association emerged from the episode looking greedy and concerned only with advancing their own selfish interests.

The public meanwhile was ready to accept the worst possible interpretation of the players' behavior. Many feel that the players make too much money anyway. So it was common during this time to hear people say that they did not care much about a group of millionaires who wanted more money than most working people would ever make in their lives. This appeal to class bias worked and helped paint the union membership, the overwhelming majority of whom were Black, as avaricious and mercenary.

On the other hand, people never seem to complain about how much money NBA owners make. No one seems concerned that NBA commissioner David Stern makes a multimillion-dollar salary himself, for that matter. The public certainly does not begrudge or resent the owners' right to make money or the commissioner's right to be compensated at such a high salary for carrying out the owners' bidding.

Billionaire owners like Paul Allen, the cofounder of Microsoft, who also owns the Portland Trail Blazers, or Howard Schultz, who owns Starbucks and the Seattle SuperSonics, are never told that they already have too much money, so their NBA earnings should and will be capped. This would be inconceivable, as these individuals are allowed to make as much money as they possibly can and indeed, are celebrated, respected, and admired for doing it. As Barzini in *The Godfather* said, "After all, we are not Communists."

In order for these owners to pay such large sums to the players, however, they must make even larger sums. This seems not to be a problem. The owners are entitled to make as much as they want without fear of reprisal. The players, by contrast, who "own" their ability and who draw the fans to the arenas and television screens, are thought to be taking money that they do not deserve, almost as though they are stealing it. Racial stereotypes are abundant in these perceptions: it is acceptable for a White billionaire to make money off of Black athletic labor, but it is not acceptable for a Black athlete to profit from his own talents and labors.

The owners can charge exorbitant ticket prices because of the talent the players bring to bear. Global corporations and wealthy individuals spend large sums to buy courtside tickets to watch basketball, again, because of the players. No fan has ever gone to a basketball game to *see* someone "coach," nor have they gone to a game to *see* someone "own." People attend basketball games and watch on television to see players do what they do best, play the game. Yet when these players attempt to discuss the circumstances around their working conditions, they are treated as greedy villains trying to destroy the American way of life and sporting tradition when indeed, they are simply behaving like capitalists of the highest order.

It is almost as though because they make so much money they should not even be allowed to complain about labor issues, even though these issues persist, even though they are important considerations. The underlying assumption here, when considering the racial implications, is that these Black players should be grateful for the mere opportunity to earn the money in the first place. The imposition of this notion, which stipulates that one "needs to be grateful," is where America's true colors, no pun intended, are quite visible.

DOIN' ME

As the players in question get to be younger and younger, it is certain that the influence of hip hop will continue to reign supreme. Hip hop at this point is more than just the music that the players listen to on their ubiquitous headphones, in the same way that basketball is more than just another game. Hip hop is a way of life that best defines the worldview from which these contemporary players emerge.

Hip hop has always been about having an upward trajectory. An abiding sense of social mobility abounds. Basketball has become the way that many who are talented enough and fortunate enough get to experience that mobility. This is their opportunity to showcase their skills and become rich in the process. What angers and alarms so many is the fact that a lot of these players have no interest whatsoever in imitating the ways of mainstream White society. This is evident in the style choices favored by so many contemporary players. Cornrows have replaced the bald head. Long baggy shorts are de rigueur. Tattoos are the order of the day.

The exception to this is a player like Tim Duncan, he of West Indian descent. West Indians have often been considered as better able to assimilate into mainstream America than their African American counterparts; think Sidney Poitier and Colin Powell, for example. Duncan then seems to be a throwback, a player from a previous time whose fundamental style of play and extremely unassuming disposition make him stand out among a league of players deeply ensconced in the hip hop milieu. No matter how much attention is lavished on Duncan by approving league and media starmakers, he is the exception, not the rule. Hip hop–minded players dominate the game and the conversations around it.

Though Duncan may be a throwback, it is a player like Rasheed Wallace who to me epitomizes the idea of retro. Wallace alternates between cornrows and a nappy old-school 'fro, also in the signature shoe of the hip hop generation, the now vintage Nike Air Force One. Wallace has also been a source of controversy throughout his tenure in the league. He was one of the first players that the league fined for wearing his shorts too long, for instance.

Obviously the length of someone's shorts has nothing to do with how he plays basketball. A player wearing long shorts does not in any way gain a competitive advantage over a player in shorter pants. As the length of all basketball shorts has gotten longer over time, the extremely long shorts are about style, and especially hip hop style. This is where the problem comes in. The NBA wants to control the players' image and suppress expression of this hip hop style on the court. The result is the enforcement of nonsensical rules about ultimately insignificant issues like the length of shorts.

John Stockton, the older White superstar of the Utah Jazz, continues to wear his shorts at the same length they were worn back in the old days. His especially "short shorts" are worn to make a statement that he is not like the younger Black players in the league. Stockton's shorts are like basketball's version of the Confederate flag; an attempt to hold on to an antiquated and outdated sense of the NBA in spite of the obvious changes that abound.

Many of the younger Black players in the league, like Rasheed Wallace, wear their shorts long to make an equally provocative statement: "This is our league, and we will do things in accordance with our culture." Early in the 2001–2002 season, several Black players, including Kobe Bryant and Shaquille O'Neal, were fined and told to make the length of their shorts conform to league standards.

Hip hop–minded players like Rasheed Wallace are constantly being criticized for other things as well. The media has tended to focus on Wallace's excessive number of technical fouls, of which admittedly there are many. Wallace's emotion on the court is a demonstration of his desire to play the game at a high level. No one knows what to do with a Black man who exhibits emotion though. Unlike others, Black men are not allowed to exhibit anything remotely approximating passion. It is too often misperceived as a violent threat. In this regard they seem to be caught in a frustrating catch-22. If someone is angry, they are too emotional. And if they are laid back, they are not angry enough.

This double standard was most clearly at work when Rasheed Wallace was called for a technical foul in a playoff game against the Lakers back in 2000. Wallace was charged with a technical for an "intimidating stare" pointed in the direction of referee Ron Garretson. Though Wallace's reputation of being given to outbursts preceded him, this call was ridiculous. The call was the equivalent of accusing Wallace of "reckless eyeballing," a Jim Crow charge often leveled against Black men when it was perceived that they had been looking at a White woman or looking in a way thought disrespectful to a White person.

Though players like Wallace have come to represent the majority of players in the league, they are often still being discussed and manipulated by people of another generation and from another disposition altogether. Gone are the days when Jackie Robinson broke the color line in baseball and Black athletes were simply content to be included. Things have now changed quite drastically. One cannot honestly discuss sports in American society without including the contributions of Black people as a primary part of that conversation. After several generations of prominent Black athletes, their significance in sports is very much like their significance in the music industry: unquestionable. These are two areas of the culture where Black people have not only excelled, but where they are the standard by which all others are measured.

This being the case, contemporary Black athletes feel no need to simply be content because they are being included. Unfortunately, their inclusion on the athletic side of things often mirrors a relative exclusion in other realms of the sporting world. Many members of the mainstream media are White and of a different generation. They often want to impose the dictates of the past on the Black athletes of the present. They tend to have the same expectations of an Allen Iverson as they did of a Joe Louis. Allen Iverson did not grow up in the same world that Joe Louis did, and he has not had the same experiences either. So why should he be expected to think and act in the same way? Contemporary Black basketball players have a great deal of money at their disposal along with a great deal of visibility and power. Yet the people who tend to control the aspects of the game off the court—the media, the league—reflect these old ideas and expectations.

I have often found that the incongruity of these circumstances is best reflected in the term "role model." To me, this is a modern-day version of saying that someone is a "credit to their race," as they said about Joe Louis and others in the past. Role model is another way of saying to the young, Black, rich and famous, "Stay in your place, speak when spoken to, and do as you are told . . . be thankful for what you've got." In response, the young, Black, rich and famous raise an extended middle finger. This seems to have resulted in an impasse. The proverbial unstoppable force meets the immovable object.

What emboldens the young, Black, rich and famous is that they know they are the reason people are paying attention in the first place. They are the reason for being. This reflects a shift in power relations. This is not to say that Black basketball players run things, but they do have a say-so. They are the attraction and they are the straws that stir the drink. Like stars in Hollywood who draw people to their movies, these basketball players command the box office. When the media, the establishment, and those fans with their heads in the sand wake up, they will realize all of this too. You cannot force a Black square peg into a round White hole. You cannot draw White blood from a Black turnip. You can however turn the game of basketball into a global entertainment commodity, with Black players at the center of a new definition of what now constitutes America.